THE BRITISH LIBRARY
writers' lives

John Keats

Ode on a Grecian Urn 1819.

1

Thou still unravish'd bride of quietness,
   Thou foster child of silence and slow time,
Sylvan Historian, who can'st thus express
   A flowery tale more sweetly than our rhyme,–
What leaf-fring'd legend haunts about thy shape,
   Of Deities, or mortals, or of both
      In Tempe, or the Dales of Arcady?
What men or Gods are these? what maidens loth?
What love? what dance? what struggle to escape?
      What pipes and timbrels? what wild extacy?

2

Heard melodies are sweet, but those unheard
   Are sweeter, – therefore ye soft pipes play on;
Not to the sensual ear, but, more endear'd,
   Pipe to the spirit–ditties of no tone;
Fair Youth, beneath the trees thou can'st not leave
   Thy song, nor ever can those trees be bare, –
      Bold lover, never, never can'st thou kiss,
Tho' winning near the goal, – O, do not grieve!
      She cannot fade, tho' thou hast not thy bliss
For ever wilt thou love, and she be fair!

THE BRITISH LIBRARY
writers' lives

John Keats

STEPHEN HEBRON

OXFORD
UNIVERSITY PRESS

❦ Contents

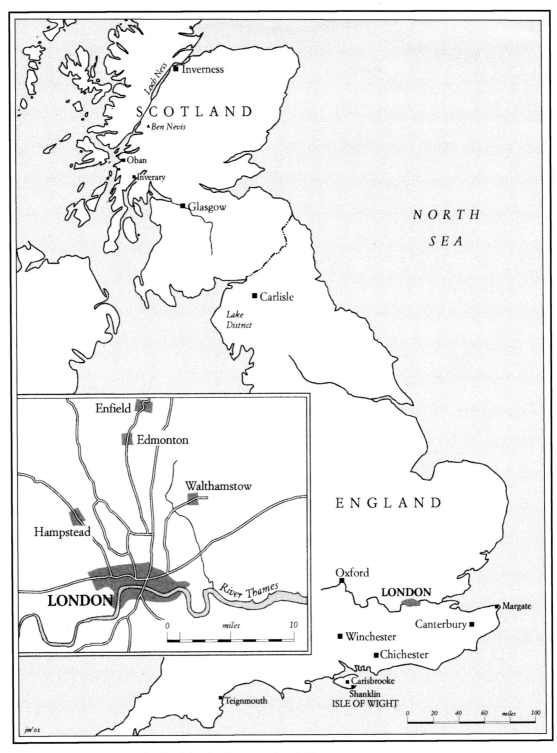

Map showing places in England and Scotland associated with Keats.

Early Life: 1795–1811

John Keats's earliest years were spent among the noisy, crowded streets of the City of London. He was born on 31 October 1795 in Moorfields, close to the Guildhall. His mother, Frances, was the daughter of John Jennings, a prosperous property owner. Little is known of his father, Thomas, beyond the fact that in 1802 he took over the management of one of his father-in-law's London properties, a busy inn and stables called the Swan and Hoop. There the seven-year-old Keats and his two younger brothers, George and Tom, went to live. A year later a sister, Fanny, was born, and Keats and George were sent to boarding school at Enfield, at that time a village ten miles north of the city.

Keats's younger brothers George (b. 1797) left and Tom (b. 1799) right, by Joseph Severn. Whereas Keats resembled their father, George and Tom, it was said, took after their mother.

Keats House, London

GIVEN BY J. PIERPONT MORGAN LL.D 1920
HAIR OF JOHN KEATS, CUT ON ⋯ DEATHBED BY JOSEPH SEVERN

GIVEN BY
THE EXECUTORS OF SIR CHARLES DILKE, 1911

JOSEPH SEVERN (1793-1879) JOHN KEATS

713

Opposite page:

A miniature of Keats in his early twenties by Joseph Severn, which was exhibited at the Royal Academy in 1819. Keats later gave the portrait to Fanny Brawne.

Fitzwilliam Museum, Cambridge

Left:

Keat's sister Fanny in middle age. A portrait by Juan Llanos.

Keats House, London

When Keats was eight his home life suddenly fell apart. In April 1804 his father died in a riding accident. Only two months after the tragedy his mother, by all accounts a rather wilful person, married again, to a man named William Rawlings. The following year his grandfather, John Jennings, died and the family quarrelled bitterly over his will. A year later, his mother separated from her second husband, and disappeared. Keats, along with his brothers and sister, were sent to live with their maternal grandmother at Ponders End near Enfield.

A drawing of Enfield School, where Keats was a pupil between 1803 and 1811. The house has since been demolished.

Sario Manicone/ Keats-Shelley House, Rome

Enfield School now became Keats's real home. Here his parents had made a good choice. While his contemporary Percy Bysshe Shelley endured flogging and bullying at Eton, Keats enjoyed a more enlightened regime. The liberal headmaster, John Clarke, cultivated a family atmosphere among the eighty or so pupils. In place of flogging he devised a system whereby each pupil kept an account book in which they entered good and bad marks according to their behaviour. Prizes were given for voluntary translations from Latin and French, and part of the large garden adjoining the playground was set aside for boys to grow their own flowers and vegetables. There was a well-stocked and varied library.

Keats's closest friend at Enfield was the headmaster's son, Charles Cowden Clarke. Clarke was eight years Keats's senior, and worked as his father's assistant. Writing his recollections many years later, he could recall little of Keats as a very young boy, except that he resembled his father, and that 'he had a brisk winning face and was a favourite with all.' As he grew older, however, Keats began to show signs of the passionate nature that would always mark him out. Though small for his age, he became famous as a fighter, and was greatly respected, remembered Clarke, for his 'terrier courage.' At times his high spirits would turn into uncontrollable anger, and on one occasion he even went so far as to challenge a teacher who had been reprimanding his brother Tom. But he also had a sensitivity and an open-heartedness that endeared him to everyone. Whether 'in passions of tears or outrageous fits of laughter' recalled a fellow pupil, Edward Holmes, he was 'always in extremes.'

When Keats was about thirteen his mother made peace with her family, and returned. Her reappearance inspired an abrupt change of attitude in her eldest son. Hitherto Keats had shown little, if any interest in academic matters. 'He was a boy', wrote Holmes, 'whom any one from his extraordinary vivacity & personal beauty might easily have fancied would become great – but rather in some military capacity than in literature.' Now, hoping no doubt to please his mother, he threw himself into work. With characteristic energy and single-mindedness he set out to read every book in the school library, and, in Cowden Clarke's words, 'carry off all the first prizes in literature.' All his time was devoted to study. While his friends were out walking or playing cricket, he would stay indoors and translate Virgil. When his exasperated teachers forced him outside to take some exercise, he would wander around the garden with a book. Even mealtimes were given over to reading: 'I see him now at supper', recalled Clarke, 'sitting back on the form, from the table, holding the volume of Burnett's History of his own Time between himself and the table, eating his meal from beyond it.' He developed a particular love for Greek mythology, and appeared to learn Lemprière's Classical Dictionary by heart.

The reunion between mother and son was, however, to be tragically brief. Frances had returned a sick woman, and by the end of 1809 she was gravely ill with tuberculosis. That Christmas Keats nursed her with an intense devotion; he cooked for her, gave her medicines, and sat up with her all night reading her novels. But there was no cure for the disease, and in March the following year she died. Keats, who by then had returned to school, was inconsolable. 'When his mother died',

remembered Holmes, 'he gave way to such impassioned & prolonged grief – (hiding himself in a nook under the master's desk) as awakened the liveliest pity and sympathy in all who saw him.'

Keats's time at Enfield was now drawing to a close. That summer, aged fourteen and a half, he left the school to begin his chosen career. He went to the neighbouring village of Edmonton, to take up an apprenticeship with an apothecary, Thomas Hammond.

~~~ *Medical Apprentice: 1811–16*

K
eats spent the next five years as an apprentice. Compared with the upheavals of his schooldays they were quiet years – 'the most placid period of his painful life' Cowden Clarke later said. The rural apothecary was the general practitioner of the day, and Keats would have observed Thomas Hammond perform any number of medical tasks: pulling teeth, setting broken limbs, delivering babies, and the most common treatment of the day, letting blood. As he grew in knowledge, Keats would have been expected to perform many of these procedures himself. Then there were the more routine chores of the apprentice: sweeping the surgery floor, bottling leeches, and mixing the numerous botanical and mineral remedies with pestle and mortar.

When he wasn't working, Keats continued to read and write with enormous energy. He completed an ambitious project he had started at school – a translation of the whole of Virgil's *Æneid*. He also began to take an interest in English poetry, and here Cowden Clarke acted as a knowledgeable and supportive guide. Once a

Edmonton in 1806. Keats was an apprentice apothecary here between 1811 and 1815.

Guildhall Library, Corporation of London

week Keats would walk the three miles to Enfield with a book in his hand for them to read. 'When the weather permitted', Clarke recalled, 'we always sat in an arbour at the end of a spacious garden, and ... had a good talk.' Keats 'devoured rather than read', and years later Clarke could still vividly recall his overwhelming delight as he discovered the great writers of the past. Edmund Spenser's *Faerie Queene* was a particular favourite – he went through it 'as a young horse would through a spring meadow – ramping!' – and his first poem, written in early 1814 was, fittingly, an 'Imitation of Spenser.' They were evenings that Keats never forgot, and some time later he would express his gratitude to Clarke in a verse letter:

> *Since I have walked with you through shady lanes*
> *That freshly terminate in open plains,*
> *And revelled in a chat that ceased not*
> *When at night-fall among your books we got:*
> *No, nor when supper came, nor after that -*
> *Nor when reluctantly I took my hat;*
> *No, nor till cordially you shook my hand*
> *Mid-way between our homes. Your accents bland*
> *Still sounded in my ears, when I no more*
> *Could hear your footsteps touch the gravelly floor.*

After five years with Hammond it was time for Keats to proceed to the next stage of his medical training. According to the new Apothecaries Act, in order to qualify as an apothecary he now had to complete six months' attendance at a hospital. Thus, on Sunday 1 October 1815, he enrolled as a student at Guy's Hospital in London. The squalid streets of Southwark were a considerable change from the lanes and meadows around Enfield and Edmonton – 'a beastly place of dirt, turnings and windings' was how Keats described it to Cowden Clarke – but he was now at the heart of the medical profession.

Guy's Hospital had been founded in 1724. Adjoining it was the much older establishment of St Thomas's, and together they formed one of the main centres in England for the practice, research and teaching of surgery. Here the lecturers were

all leaders in their field. Keats was taught chemistry by Alexander Marcet, a prominent Swiss chemist and fellow of the Royal Society; for the theory and practice of Medicine he attended courses by William Babington, later a President of the Geological Society, and James Curry, a fluent and knowledgeable speaker. Lectures in anatomy and physiology were given by Astley Cooper. A remarkable figure, Cooper was the most innovative surgeon of his day. His energy was enormous – 'If I laid my head upon my pillow at night without having dissected something in the day' he later remarked, 'I would think that a wasted day' – and his reputation as a

Guy's Hospital by Wallis after Shepherd, where Keats studied medicine in 1815–16.

Guildhall Library, Corporation of London

A portrait by Sir
Thomas Lawrence
of the great surgeon
Sir Astley Cooper,
Keats's lecturer in
anatomy at St. Thomas's
Hospital, London.

Royal College of Surgeons,
London

teacher second to none. 'Loud and continued greetings most truly declared the affectionate regard his pupils had for him', wrote John Flint South, a contemporary of Keats. 'His clear silvery voice and cheery conversational manner soon exhausted the conventional hour devoted to the lecture; and all who heard him hung with silent attention on his words, the only sounds which broke the quiet being the subdued pen-scratching of the note-takers.' Keats kept the notes he made from Cooper's lectures all his life.

Complementing the lecture courses was practical work. Keats was required to accompany the surgeons as they made their rounds of the wards, and to attend regular sessions in the dissecting room. Here, particularly in summer, the stench could be almost unbearable, and in order to meet the constant demand for new corpses the hospital would sometimes employ the services of grave robbers, or 'resurrection men.' On Fridays, the students would observe operations. The horrors of the pre-anaesthetic operating theatre have been vividly described by Flint South:

> *The operating theatre was small, and the rush and scuffle to get a place was not unlike that for a seat in the pit or gallery of a dramatic theatre; and when one was lucky enough to get a place, the crowding and squeezing was oftentimes unbearable ... I have often known even the floor so crowded that the surgeon could not operate till it had been partially cleared ... I soon got over the blood-shedding which necessarily ensued; and so long as the patient did not make much noise I got on very well, but if the cries were great and especially if they came from a child, I was quickly upset, had to leave the theatre, and not infrequently fainted.*

The Old Operating Theatre at St. Thomas's Hospital. The Latin sign reads 'For compassion not for gain'.

St. Thomas's Hospital, London

Hospital life required strong nerves, but Keats seems to have thrived, for in March 1816 he was made a dresser. It was a rapid promotion, and the responsibilities of the post were considerable. He now had to undertake night shifts, dealing with numerous accidents and emergencies as they came in. He also had to assist a senior surgeon in major operations. Here, unfortunately, he was appointed to work under William Lucas, an amiable man, but a horrifyingly incompetent surgeon, and as dresser it would have been Keat's task to make the best of the damage Lucas did and to bandage the wounds.

Despite the demands of his medical duties, Keats still found time for reading and, increasingly, writing. His housemate and fellow student, Henry Stephens, later recalled how during lectures 'he would sit & instead of copying the lecture, would often scribble some doggerel rhymes, among the notes of the lecture.' Through his brother George he became friends with George Felton Matthew, a very minor sentimental poet and a member of a poetry circle. Cowden Clarke continued to act as his guide to writers past and present, introducing him to the work of Leigh Hunt, a contemporary poet whose verse would come to have a considerable influence on his own writing. On 1 May 1816 one of Keats's earliest surviving poems, a sonnet entitled 'To Solitude', was published in the *Examiner*, the weekly liberal newspaper edited by Hunt.

Two months later, Keats completed the next stage of his medical training. On 25 July he sat, and passed, an examination at Apothecaries Hall. This examination had been established as part of the 1815 Apothecaries Act. It was intended to ensure high standards in the profession, and so distinguish apothecaries from, in Flint South's words, 'old women and quacks for which the public had long had great propensity.' Keats had to demonstrate considerable knowledge of materia medica (the compounding of drugs), pharmaceutical chemistry, and the theory and practice of medicine. It was a searching exam, and he did well to pass.

After the examination Keats went with his brother, Tom, to the seaside resort of Margate on the Kent coast, for a well-deserved rest. He stayed until September, then returned to London and took new lodgings in Southwark with his brothers. He had shown considerable aptitude as a student, and the logical next step, now that he had qualified as an apothecary, was to continue his training and become a surgeon.

Keats's first published poem, 'To Solitude', in The Examiner, *5 May 1816.*

The British Library, London

THE EXAMINER.

262

tions after MONMOUTH's enterprise: or, to adopt the case properly mentioned by Sir FRANCIS BURDETT, from the miscreants, clothed in ermine, who murdered those martyrs and ornaments of their age, RUSSELL and SYDNEY. Mr. LAW's legal reading and knowledge of history and facts must be miserably defective if he does not see a necessity for the fear he deprecates, and if he does not recognize in Parliament a court holding jurisdiction over every other court, capable not only of investigating judicial proceedings, but also of sending to impeachment and chastisement every Judge in the kingdom. Judges, like other men, are fallible; and we have seen that even the voice of conscience, and the solemnity of oaths, have yielded to the baleful influence of bad circumstances. What then remains but the fear of public opinion and Parliamentary inquiry? Has Mr. LAW to be told, that if fear takes away the judgment, so do flattery of and fawning on the Great. Let us suppose a Judge the constant attendant at levees, the haunter of palaces, a man of aspiring ambition, anxious to aggrandize himself and family,—take away the fear of Parliamentary enquiry from such a Judge and he may become the compliant sycophant and mere tool of power, eager to stretch royal prerogative and invade public right, the partaker of indecent orgies, and the minister of vengeance on such as denounce despotism and its vices—the base prototype of Cambyses' Judges, who when their approbation was demanded by the Prince to some illegal measure, said that though there was a written law, the Persian Kings might follow their own will and pleasure.

"Our suspicions respecting Sweden were not without foundation. A war between that country and Denmark is hinted at in the French papers. The journey of the Ex-King to the North is doubtless connected with this state of affairs, and we should not be at all surprised to see M. BERNADOTTE follow the example of the other Potentates whom the French Revolution raised from obscurity to thrones."—*Sun.*

Besides Count TORRENO, five or six other Spaniards have been arrested at Paris. It is also said, that all the Spanish refugees in France, who reside in Provinces adjoining to Spain, have been ordered to retire into the interior of the kingdom.

They write from the Hague, that the French Refugees have received orders to retire to the towns situated in the northern parts of the Netherlands.

The republic of letters has just sustained a loss by the death of Sir HERBERT CROFT, who lived in France for the last 15 years.

An Extraordinary Gazette of the Government of Lima, dated the 23d of December, 1815, contains a dispatch from PEZUELA, the General in Chief of the army of Upper Peru, in which he boasts of having obtained a complete victory over RONDEAU, who commands the army of the Buenos Ayres rebels, as they are called.

On Friday a Special Court of Common Council was held at Guildhall, when Mr. Alderman BIRCH moved an Address to the PRINCE REGENT, congratulating him on the Marriage of the Princess CHARLOTTE with the Prince of COBOURG; another Address of a similar nature to the QUEEN; and the compliments and congratulations of the Court to the Princess CHARLOTTE, and to the Prince of COBOURG, separately. The motion was unanimously agreed to.

A letter has appeared, Signed "Jos. JACKSON," relative to the West India Colonies and the Appointment of Agents in this country. Upon this letter, and upon Colonial affairs in general, we shall shortly have something to communicate, which will abundantly prove, that the system now established is founded in deception, corruption, and injustice.

Some foreign Papers have alluded to a Note, addressed by the Court of Rome to the Minister Plenipotentiary of the King of the Netherlands, approving the conduct of the Belgic Prelates, in refusing to accept certain Articles of the new Ecclesiastical Constitution.

A letter dated Verona, April 10, speaking of the death of the Empress of AUSTRIA, says, "One cannot make too public the noble and affecting scene that the last moments of the Empress presented. This august Princess desired to see successively, in private, all the persons of her household; she addressed to each of them words of kindness and consolation. She expressed some satisfaction that the Archduchess BEATRICE, her mother, was accidentally at a distance from a scene which would have too deeply affected her heart.—" The road to the tomb," said the dying Princess, " is that of truth; all illusions cease; there is no more flattery, there is no more grandeur; it must be forgotten that I have been Empress and Queen. I wish that people may retain of me sentiments honourable to my memory." Her MAJESTY desired to embrace the Ladies who approached the nearest to her, and the following were the last words that could be collected :—" Happiness is in a good conscience: I feel this soothing sentiment much more in death than upon the Throne.—Adieu! my friends! my children! Adieu!"—She ceased to breathe."

To the City Address respecting the French Protestants, the PRINCE REGENT has returned the following " most gracious" Answer :—

" The just sense entertained by his Majesty's subjects of the value and importance of Religious Toleration is necessarily calculated to excite in their minds strong feeling of uneasiness and regret at any appearance of the want of it in other nations of the world.—In such feelings, when called for and justified by the occasion, I shall ever participate ; and, whilst I lament the circumstances which led to your Address, I derive great satisfaction from the persuasion that they are in no degree to be attributed to an indisposition on the part of the Government of France to afford to the freedom of Religious Worship the benefit of its promised protection and support."

A letter has been forwarded to us respecting the death of a soldier, named *Hegg*, belonging to the 3d regiment of Guards. The Writer asserts, that the Sister of the deceased, on visiting him in the hospital, was told by him, that he had received an injury in his arm, and that he should not see her any more. He died soon after. Previous to this, he had complained of severe pain in his arm, which he attributed to the extent of the incision made when he was bled, which is described in the letter as being large enough to admit the first joint of the little finger. The Writer says, it has been given out that hard drinking occasioned Hegg's death ; but this he strongly denies; and he adds, that the Sister of the deceased was refused admittance to see the remains, till the body was so changed that she with difficulty recognised it to be her brother's, and the blood was then oozing through the shroud.

TO SOLITUDE.

O SOLITUDE! if I must with thee dwell,
 Let it not be among the jumbled heap
 Of murky buildings ;—climb with me the steep,
Nature's Observatory—whence the dell,
Its flowery slopes—its rivers crystal swell,
 May seem a span ; let me thy vigils keep
 'Mongst boughs pavilioned ; where the Deer's swift leap
Startles the wild Bee from the Fox-glove bell.
Ah ! fain would I frequent such scenes with thee ;
 But the sweet converse of an innocent mind,
 Whose words are images of thoughts refin'd,
Is my soul's pleasure ; and it sure must be
 Almost the highest bliss of human kind,
When to thy haunts two kindred spirits flee.
                                                        J. K

On the first looking into Chapman's Homer

Much have I have ell'd in the Realms of Gold,
And many goodly States, and Kingdoms seen;
Round many Western islands have I been,
Which Bards in featty to Apollo hold.
Of one wide expanse had I been told,
Which deep brow'd Homer ruled as his Demesne:
Yet could I never judge what Men could mean,
Till I heard Chapman speak out loud and bold.
Then felt I like some Watcher of the Skies
When a new Planet swims into his Ken,
Or like stout Cortez, when with wond'ring eyes
He star'd at the Pacific, and all his Men
Look'd at each other with a wild surmise —
Silent upon a Peak in Darien —

The manuscript of 'On First looking into Chapman's Homer' (1816). Keats wrote this, his first great poem, after reading George Chapman's translation of Homer with Cowden Clarke.

The Houghton Library, Harvard University, Massachusetts

Poetry, however, had now become an essential part of his life, and he began to realise that here he might have real ability. Sometime in October, Cowden Clarke was lent a rare folio edition of George Chapman's translation of Homer, and one evening he and Keats read it together until well into the night. Towards dawn they parted, and when Clarke came downstairs to breakfast later in the morning he was astonished to find a letter from Keats containing the sonnet 'On first looking into Chapman's Homer.' Keats had written this, his first indisputably great poem, immediately on returning home, and had sent it to Clarke by messenger:

Much have I travell'd in the Realms of Gold,

And many goodly States and Kingdoms seen,

Round many Western islands have I been

Which Bards in fealty to Apollo hold.

Oft of one wide expanse had I been told,

Which deep brow'd Homer ruled as his Demesne:

Yet could I never judge what Men could mean,

Till I heard Chapman speak out loud and bold.

Then felt I like some Watcher of the Skies

When a new Planet swims into his Ken,

Or like stout Cortez, when with wond'ring eyes

He star'd at the Pacific, and all his Men

Look'd at each other with a wild surmise –

Silent upon a Peak in Darien.

 *Apprentice Poet: 1816–17*

'On first looking into Chapman's Homer' heralded a new stage in Keats's career. Over the next few months he would be given a captivating taste of the contemporary literary world, and what is more would be hailed by people he admired as a young writer of exceptional promise. Henceforth poetry, not medicine, would be the guiding force in his life. His one ambition would be to live as a poet.

Shortly after their evening with Chapman's Homer, Cowden Clarke offered to introduce Keats to Leigh Hunt. Hunt had found fame in 1814 when he and his brother John had been sentenced to two years imprisonment for a libel on the Prince

The poet and liberal journalist Leigh Hunt, by Thomas Charles Wageman.

National Portrait Gallery, London

Regent. He was a man of great personal charm who managed to combine a chaotic domestic life with a unique capacity for enjoyment, and as he later said in his *Autobiography*, a 'tendency to reap pleasure from every object in creation.' He had furnished his prison cell with a piano, bookcases and engravings, and had tastefully concealed the bars on the windows with Venetian blinds. His visitors had included not only the Clarkes (who had kept him supplied with fresh fruit and vegetables) but also the philosopher Jeremy Bentham, the writer Charles Lamb, and the poet Lord Byron, who described him to his friend Thomas Moore as 'a good man, with some poetical elements in his chaos.' On his release in October 1815 (an event which Keats, while still at Edmonton, had celebrated in a sonnet) he had moved into a cottage in the Vale of Health on Hampstead Heath north of London, and his natural cheerfulness had quickly turned the house into a hub of literary and artistic life. It was here, the following October, that Cowden Clarke offered to take Keats.

A view by George Shepherd of the Vale of Health on Hampstead Heath (1825). Leigh Hunt had a cottage here and Keats was a frequent visitor.

Victoria & Albert Museum, London

''Twill be an era in my existence' Keats replied, and when the day came, he could barely suppress his excitement. 'The character and expression of Keats's features would arrest even the casual passenger in the street', Clarke later wrote, 'and now they were wrought to a tone of the animation that I could not but watch with interest ... As we approached the Heath, there was the rising and accelerated step, with the gradual subsidence of all talk.'

Hunt took to Keats immediately. 'We became intimate on the spot', he later wrote, 'and I found the young poet's heart as warm as his imagination.' His response to the poems that Keats had brought with him was also typically enthusiastic: 'I shall never forget the impression made upon me by the exuberant specimens of genuine though young poetry that were laid before me.' Over the coming months he would do much to promote and support his new disciple.

That same month Clarke offered to introduce Keats to the painter Benjamin Robert Haydon. 'I shall be punctual as the Bee to the Clover', Keats told him. 'Very glad am I at the thought of meeting this glorious Haydon and all his creation.'

The historical painter Benjamin Robert Haydon by David Wilkie.

National Portrait Gallery, London

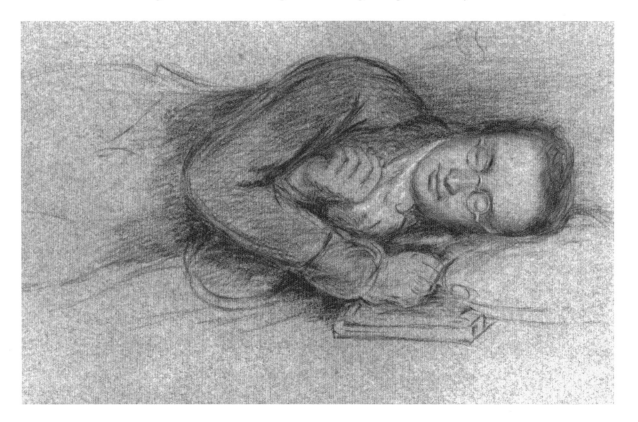

Haydon was a very different character from Hunt. A man of great seriousness and gigantic ambition, he eschewed the more profitable practice of portrait painting in favour of vast canvasses portraying heroic episodes from history and the Bible. With his ambition came an intense egoism, and a remarkable capacity for violent hatred, but he was also a generous man with a considerable gift for friendship. Though he self-consciously cast himself in the role of genius, he was also happy to recognise genius in others, and he saw it in Keats. 'He is a sound young man & will be a great one', he noted in his diary, adding characteristically, 'The interest I excite amongst the genius of the Country is certainly very singular. There must be something in me too.' The two men soon became intimate, supporting each other in their hopes, and sharing some of their most private doubts. 'Keats is really & truly the man after my own heart' Haydon wrote. 'We saw through each other *at once*, and I hope in God we are friends for ever.'

John Hamilton Reynolds by Joseph Severn.

National Portrait Gallery, London

Through Haydon, Keats met John Hamilton Reynolds. Of the same age as Keats, Reynolds was then working as a junior clerk in an insurance office. To Keats he was 'the playfullest' of his friends, 'slovenly in dress', 'inspired by Mercury', a man who 'makes you laugh and yet think.' 'He was the most good-natured fellow I ever met with', wrote the poet John Clare in his *Sketches*, 'his face was the three-in-one of fun wit and punning personified.' But Reynolds was also fellow writer who already had four publications to his name, someone with whom Keats would, over the coming years, share his most profound thoughts about writing and poetry.

On 31 October Keats celebrated his twenty-first birthday. The following month he moved with his brothers into a house on Cheapside in east London, and with the

move came a sense of domestic security which he expressed in a touching sonnet, 'To my Brothers':

> Small busy flames play through the fresh laid coals,
> And their faint cracklings o'er our silence creep
> Like whispers of the household gods that keep
> A gentle empire o'er fraternal souls.

Soon afterwards he sent another sonnet to Haydon, 'Great Spirits now on Earth are sojourning', which, more than anything, conveys the exhilaration and excitement of this period of his life. In it he praised his three 'great spirits': Haydon himself, Hunt, and the major contemporary poet whose work he had recently discovered, William Wordsworth.

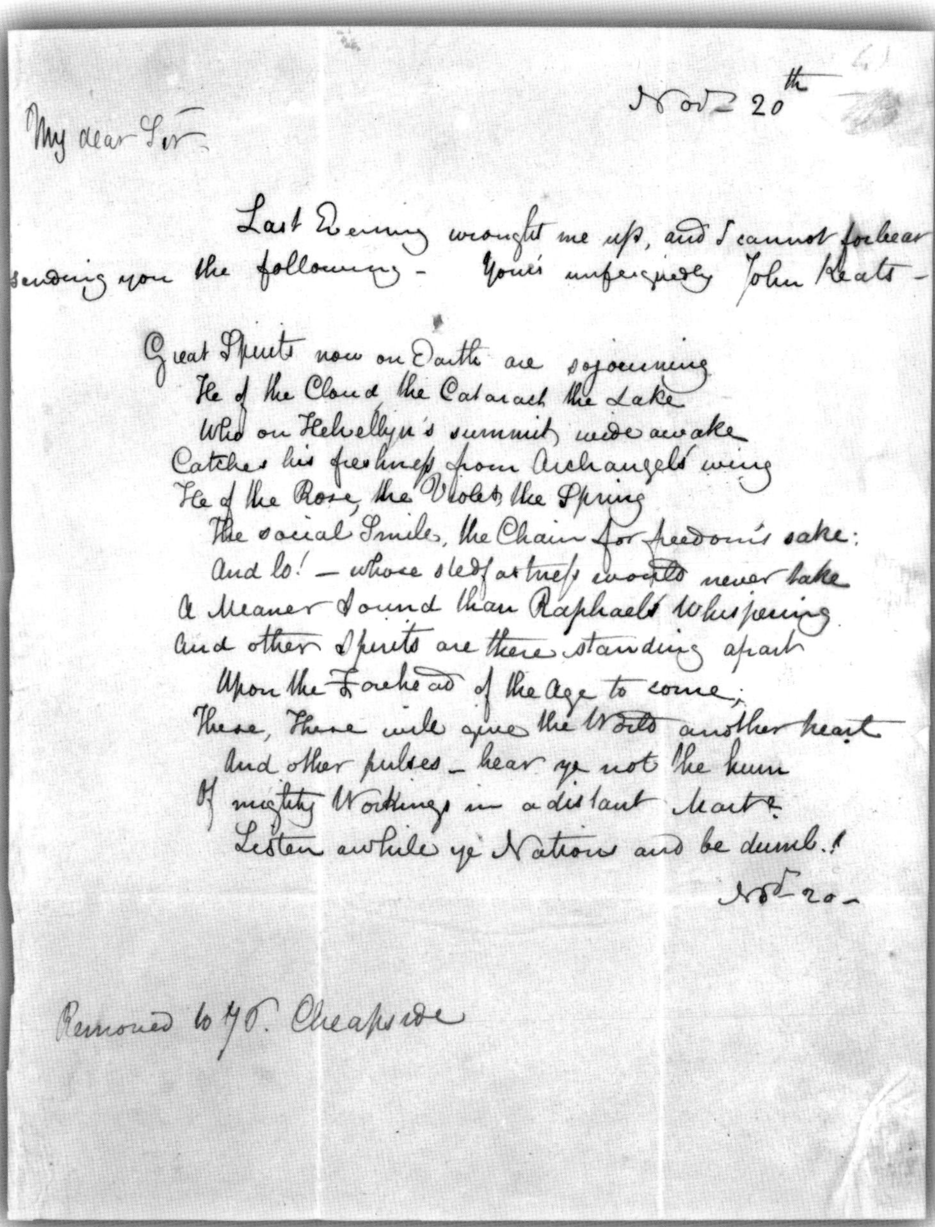

My dear Sir

Nov 20th

Last Evening wrought me up, and I cannot forbear sending you the following — Yours unfeignedly John Keats —

Great Spirits now on Earth are sojourning
He of the Cloud, the Cataract the Lake
Who on Helvellyn's summit wide awake
Catches his freshness from Archangel's wing
He of the Rose, the Violet, the Spring
The social Smile, the Chain for freedom's sake:
And lo! — whose stedfastness would never take
A Meaner Sound than Raphael's Whispering
And other Spirits are there standing apart
Upon the Forehead of the Age to come;
These, these will give the World another heart
And other pulses — hear ye not the hum
Of mighty Workings in a distant Mart?
Listen awhile ye Nations and be dumb.!

Nov 20 —

Removed to 76. Cheapside

A letter from Keats to Haydon, 20 November 1816, containing the sonnet 'Great Spirits', which Haydon later sent to Wordsworth.

The Houghton Library, Harvard University, Massachusetts

27

Haydon offered to send the poem on to Wordsworth himself; 'The Idea of your sending it to Wordsworth put me out of breath', Keats replied. 'You know with what Reverence – I would send my well wishes to him.'

In this intoxicating atmosphere Keats finally determined to give up medicine altogether and, as he told Haydon, 'fix my eye on one horizon.' After his grandmother's death at the end of 1814 he, his brothers and sister had been placed in the care of guardians. Keats now resolved to tell the surviving guardian, Richard Abbey, of his decision. Abbey, a tea merchant without literary interests, was appalled; their conversation was later reported by Keats's publisher, John Taylor:

He communicated his plans to his Ward but his Surprise was not moderate, to hear in Reply, that he did not intend to be a Surgeon – Not intend to be a Surgeon? why what do you mean to be? I mean to rely upon my Abilities as a Poet – John, you are either Mad or a Fool, to talk in so absurd a Manner. My Mind is made up, said the youngster very quietly. I know that I possess Abilities greater than most Men, and therefore I am determined to gain my Living by exercising them.

On 1 December 1816 Leigh Hunt introduced Keats to the public. In an article in the *Examiner* he grouped together three 'Young Poets' of special promise: Percy Bysshe Shelley, Reynolds, and Keats; 'He has not published anything except in a newspaper', Hunt wrote of Keats, 'but a set of his manuscripts was handed us the other day, and further surprised us with the truth of their ambition, and ardent grappling with Nature.' He then went on to quote 'On first looking into Chapman's Homer' in full. Henry Stephens later recalled the pleasure that Keats derived from this article: 'This sealed his fate and he gave himself up more completely than before to poetry.'

Further compliments followed. Two weeks after Hunt's article, Haydon made a life mask of Keats's features. He had decided to introduce him into the crowd of his current historical painting, 'Christ's Triumphal Entry into Jerusalem', and made the mask in preparation. A friend from his time at Guy's, Joseph Severn, also recorded his features in a charcoal sketch. Though at five foot and three quarters of an inch Keats was physically small, his eager, upright stance and dynamic manner gave him considerable presence. It was his

Haydon made this lifemask of Keats in 1816.

Wordsworth Trust, Grasmere

expression that particularly struck Severn; it was, the artist later said, 'peculiarly dauntless … such as may be seen in the face of some seamen', and after the poet's death he could still picture 'those falcon-eyes … the almost flamelike intensity of Keats's eager glances when he was keenly excited or interested.' With this intensity came a gift for observation that Severn noticed on their walks around Hampstead Heath:

> *Nothing seemed to escape him, the song of a bird and the undernote of response from covert or hedge, the rustle of some animal, the changing of the green and brown lights and furtive shadows, the motions of the wind – just how it took certain tall flowers and plants – and the wayfaring of the clouds: even the features and gestures of passing tramps, the colour of one woman's hair, the smile on one child's face, the furtive animalism below the deceptive humanity in many of the vagrants, even the hats, clothes, shoes, wherever these conveyed the remotest hint as to the real self of the wearer.*

In February 1817 two further sonnets by Keats, 'To Kosciusko' and 'After dark vapours', were published in the *Examiner*. Then, at the beginning of March, his first collection, *Poems*, was published by Charles Ollier. The volume included a number of sonnets, including 'On first looking into Chapman's Homer' and 'Great spirits on earth are sojourning', together with verse epistles to his brothers, George Felton Matthew and Cowden Clarke. There were also two longer works: 'I stood tiptoe on a little hill', the opening poem, described the landscape of his boyhood and the scenery around Hampstead; 'Sleep and Poetry', partly written on a sofa bed set up for his use at the Vale of Health, was his first attempt to write in a more philosophical vein, and closed the volume. Both, with their chatty tone, easy style and prettiness of imagery, betray the influence of Hunt, and show that Keats was yet to find his own voice in more ambitious poems. Overall, the volume contains few signs of the great work that was to follow, but it stands as a fitting memorial to Keats's first, discovering steps as a poet.

A fragment from the original manuscript of Keats's poem 'I stood tiptoe on a little hill', written in 1816.

The British Library, London
Zweig MS 163 f.1

Poems,

BY

JOHN KEATS.

" What more felicity can fall to creature,
" Than to enjoy delight with liberty."
Fate of the Butterfly.—SPENSER.

LONDON:

PRINTED FOR

C. & J. OLLIER, 3, WELBECK STREET,

CAVENDISH SQUARE.

1817.

~ Endymion: *1817*

K eats's friends had high hopes for *Poems*. 'The first volume of Keats's minor muse was launched amid the cheers and fond anticipations of all his circle', Cowden Clarke later wrote. 'Everyone expected (and not unreasonably) that it would create a sensation in the literary world.' 'I have read your Sleep & Poetry', enthused Haydon in a letter, 'it is a flash of lightening that will sound men from their occupations and keep them trembling for the crash of thunder that *will* follow.' As it turned out, however, the book attracted little interest and barely sold. 'Alas!', wrote Clarke, 'the book might have emerged in Timbuctoo with far stronger chance of fame and approbation.' When Keats took the book to his guardian Abbey he received a predictably blunt response: 'Well John I have read your Book, & it reminds me of the Quaker's Horse which was hard to catch, & good for nothing when he was caught – So your Book is hard to understand & good for nothing when it is understood.'

But the book had at least one significant admirer. Shortly after its appearance Keats met the publisher and bookseller John Taylor. With his partner, James Hessey, Taylor ran his business on sound commercial lines, but he also had a feeling for contemporary literature and loved to encourage new talent; John Clare,

A portrait of Keats's publisher and friend John Taylor, by Joseph Severn.

Keats House, London

The sonnet 'This pleasant tale is like a little copse', written by Keats in Cowden Clarke's copy of Chaucer's poems.

The British Library, London Add. MS 33516 f.150v

104   THE FLOURE AND THE LEAFE.

Madam, quod I, although I left worthy,
Unto the Lefe I ow mine obfervaunce.
That is, quod fhe, right well done certainly,
And I pray God to honour you advaunce,
And kepe you fro the wickid remembraunce
Of Malèbouch and all his cruiltie,
And all that gode and well-condition'd be ;   581
    For here I may no lengir now abide,
But I muft follow the grete company
That ye may fe yondir before you ride ;
And forthwith as I couth moft humily
I toke my leve of her, and fhe gan hie
Aftir them as faft as evir fhe might,
And I drow homeward, for it was nigh night,   588
    And put all that I had fene in writing,
Undir fupport of them that luft it rede.
O little boke ! thou art fo unconning,
How darft thou put thy felf in prees for drede ?
It is wondir that thou wexift not rede,
Sith that thou woft full lite who fhall behold
Thy rude langage full boyftoufly unfold.   595

Finis.

This pleasant Tale is like a little copse
    The honied lines do freshly interlace
    To keep the Reader in so sweet a place
So that he here and there full-hearted stops
And oftentimes he feels the dewy drops
    Come cool and suddenly against his face
    And by the wandring Melody may trace
Which way the tender-legged linnet hops
O what a Power hath white Simplicity!
    What mighty Power has this gentle Story
    I that for ever feel athirst for glory
Could at this Moment be content to lie

William Hazlitt and Thomas De Quincey would all come to be on his list. By April he had offered to act as Keats's publisher. 'We have agreed for the next Edit. of Keats's poems', he wrote to his father. 'I cannot feel he will fail to become a great poet.' He and Hessey bought up a number of unsold copies of *Poems*, and advanced their new author some money. Taylor had also been struck by his new author's unconventional dress; according to Henry Stephens, Keats was at this time adopting a rather Byronic pose: 'the collar turned down & a ribbon tied round his neck without any neckerchief. He also let his moustachios grow occasionally.'

Shortly after his meeting with Taylor, Keats moved with his brothers from Cheapside to the more congenial surroundings of Well Walk, on the edge of Hampstead Heath. He had an idea for a new poem. The subject was to be the Greek legend of Endymion, the shepherd from Mount Latmos who fell in love with Cynthia, the Moon, and it was to be a long work, on an altogether more ambitious scale than sonnets and verse epistles – a true test of his abilities as a poet. His brothers, always quick to support his endeavours, encouraged him to spend some time alone to begin the poem. 'My Brothers are anxious that I shod go by myself into the country', he told Reynolds on 17 March, '… they have always been extremely fond of me; and now that Haydon has pointed out how necessary it is that I shoud be alone to improve myself, they give up the temporary pleasure of living with me continually for a great good which I hope will follow.' And so, a month later, on 14 April 1817, he left the familiar surroundings of Hampstead for the Isle of Wight.

After a cold journey south, mostly spent, to save expense, on the outside of the coach, Keats arrived at Southampton. He felt rather lonely at breakfast, so he got out one of the volumes of Shakespeare's works that he had taken with him – 'there's my comfort' he wrote to his brothers. After breakfast he strolled around the town a little, then he took the ferry across the Solent to the Isle of Wight. He spent the night at Newport, and the next day moved on to the coastal village of Shanklin. The scenery enchanted him – 'Shanklin is a most beautiful place', he wrote to Reynolds, 'sloping wood and meadow ground reaches round the Chine, which is a cleft between the Cliffs of the depth of nearly 300 feet at least. This cleft is filled with trees & bushes in the narrow part; and as it widens becomes bare, if it were not for primroses on one side, which spread to the very verge of the Sea, and some fishermen's huts on the

Following pages:

Keats was enchanted by the scenery of Shanklin on the Isle of Wight, as seen in this painting by William Turner of Oxford.

Victoria & Albert Museum, London

35

other, perched midway in the Ballustrades of beautiful green Hedges along their steps down to the sands. – But the sea, Jack, the sea – the little waterfall – then the white cliff – then St Catherine's Hill – "the little sheep in the meadows, the cows in the corn".' He debated whether to take lodgings here, but in the end settled on Carisbrooke, which was both more convenient and, he told Reynolds, half the price. From his room he had a view of the medieval ruins of Carisbrooke Castle, and he soon found wooded lanes and copses to walk in. 'I intend to walk over the island east-West-North South', he told Reynolds. 'I have not seen many specimens of ruins – I dont think however I shall ever see one to surpass Carisbrooke Castle.'

But his real purpose in coming to the Isle of Wight was to write poetry, and he set about establishing his workplace. He unpacked his books and put them in a corner, and hung some pictures he had brought with him above his desk. He came across a portrait of Shakespeare in a passageway, and managed to persuade his landlady to let him have it for his room. It seemed a good omen, for Keats had come to venerate Shakespeare above all other writers. He read him constantly, and quotations from the plays fill his letters. And yet, as he sat alone in his room, trying to begin *Endymion*, he confessed to Reynolds that he was becoming 'rather *narvus*.' Shakespeare's towering greatness as a poet haunted him, and brooding obsessively upon his own work he could see only lack of achievement. 'I find I cannot exist without poetry', he told Reynolds, 'without eternal poetry – half the day will not do – the whole of it – I began with a little, but habit has made me a Leviathan – I had become all in a Tremble from not having written any thing of late – the Sonnet over leaf did me some good. I slept the better last night for it – this Morning, however, I am nearly as bad again.'

The remoteness, the unaccustomed solitude, the sudden realisation of the giant task ahead of him – it all seems to have become too much, and after only a week at Carisbrooke, Keats left the Isle of Wight. He headed for the familiar surroundings of Margate, and was soon joined there by his brother Tom. It had been a sobering experience, and as he reflected upon it over the next few weeks Keats wrote a number of revealing letters. The first was to Leigh Hunt: 'I went to the Isle of Wight …' he said, 'thought so much about Poetry so long together that I could not get to sleep at night … Another thing I was too much in Solitude, and consequently was obliged to be in continual burning of thought as an only resource.'

Then he wrote a more personal letter to Haydon, in which he admitted that he was depressed, and haunted by the fear of failure: 'truth is I have been in such a state of Mind as to read over my Lines and hate them … the Cliff of Poesy towers above me.' There was, he knew, a darker side to his normally vivacious character,

A letter from Keats to Leigh Hunt, 10 May 1817. Keats has signed himself 'Junkets', evidently a nickname among his friends.

The British Library, London
Ashley MS 4869 ff1, 2

one which threatened future success: 'truth is I have a horrid Morbidity of temperament which has shown itself at intervals …' he told Haydon, 'it is I have no doubt the greatest Enemy and stumbling block I have to fear – I may even say that it is likely to be the cause of my disappointment.' But his fundamental belief in himself as a poet remained. Before he left Carisbrooke his landlady had given him the portrait of Shakespeare, and Keats's thoughts turned again to his great predecessor: 'I hope for the support of a High Power while I climb this little eminence and especially in my Years of more momentous Labour', he wrote. 'I remember your saying that you had notions of a good Genius presiding over you... Is it too daring to Fancy Shakespeare this Presider?'

At Margate he began to work in earnest on the first book of *Endymion*, and his mood gradually improved. On 17 May he and Tom left for Canterbury, the ancient cathedral town further along the coast. 'This Evening I go to Canterbury', he told Taylor and Hessey. 'I was not right in my head when I came. – At Canterbury I hope the Remembrance of Chaucer will set me forward like a Billiard-Ball.' He also wrote a letter to his brother George in which he further articulated his intentions in writing *Endymion*. The idea of poetical fame, he said, was still 'towering high' above him, but he knew that he had no right to think of himself in those terms until *Endymion* was finished; 'it will be a test,' he said, 'a trial of my Powers of Imagination and chiefly of my invention which is a rare thing indeed – by which I must make 4000 Lines of one bare circumstance and fill them with Poetry.' Full of epic ambitions – 'Did our great Poets ever write short Pieces?' he asked George – Keats was instinctively turning away from the light-hearted world of Hunt, and towards the weightier aspirations of Haydon. He now remembered with some embarrassment an incident at Hampstead, when he and Hunt had composed sonnets in friendly competition, and afterwards had jokingly crowned each other with laurels. When two female callers arrived Hunt had quickly removed his 'crown', but Keats had stubbornly kept his on. It was precisely this kind of playful poeticising that he was now trying to avoid.

After a few days in Canterbury, Tom left for London. Keats meanwhile went on to Bo-Peep, a small seaside village near Hastings on the south coast, where he made the acquaintance of a woman who would turn up unexpectedly later in his life, Mrs Isabella Jones. In June he returned to Well Walk and began the second book of *Endymion*. That summer he worked steadily on the poem, and when not occupied in composition would take walks over Hampstead Heath with Severn and Reynolds. He also forged a number of new friendships. Close to Well Walk was Wentworth Place, an attractive, recently built house named after its co-owner, Charles Wentworth Dilke. Six years older than Keats, Dilke worked as a clerk at the Navy Pay Office in Somerset House, and had literary interests; between 1814

Three of Keats's London friends. Left to right: Charles Wentworth Dilke, James Rice and Benjamin Bailey.

Keats House, London

and 1816 he had published a six-volume edition of *Old English Plays*. He and his wife Maria became loyal and sensitive friends, and in the coming months Wentworth Place was something like a second home to Keats and his brothers. Sharing ownership of the house with Dilke was Charles Armitage Brown, who according to his custom was currently letting his side of the house for the summer while he toured his native Scotland.

Through Reynolds Keats met James Rice, a young lawyer who, though incurably ill, had a warm humour and a philosophical outlook that made him particularly lovable – 'the most sensible, and even wise Man I know', Keats said. Also through Reynolds he met Benjamin Bailey, an Oxford undergraduate studying for ordination. Bailey shared Keats's love of literature, and the two men quickly became friends. Towards the end of the summer Bailey invited Keats to spend the second half of the vacation with him in Oxford. Keats, whose brothers had just left for France to enjoy a holiday at his expense, immediately accepted.

He arrived at Oxford at the beginning of September. Bailey lived at Magdalen Hall, and his rooms had a fine view overlooking the deer park. Keats took to the ancient university town at once; 'This Oxford I have no doubt is the finest City in the world,' he wrote to his sister Fanny, 'it is full of old Gothic buildings – Spires – towers – Quadrangles – Cloisters Groves &c and is surrounded with more Clear streams than ever I saw together. I take a walk by the side of one of them every Evening and thank God, we have not had a drop of Rain these many days.' Fanny was then fourteen, still under Abbey's guardianship, and living a rather lonely life at a boarding school in Walthamstow outside London. Keats, who was deeply fond of his sister, saw far less of her than he would have liked. He now proposed that they write to each other regularly: 'Let us now begin a regular question and answer, a little pro and con; letting it interfere as a pleasant method of my coming at your favorite little wants and enjoyments, that I may meet them in a way befitting a brother.'

Bailey and Keats quickly established a methodical working pattern. After breakfast Bailey would settle down to his studies, while Keats would sit across the room and work on Book III of *Endymion*. He wrote rapidly – some fifty lines a day – 'with as much regularity, & apparently with as much ease,' Bailey later recalled, 'as he wrote his letters.' But he was growing tired of the poem; his thoughts were developing all the time, and he was keen to get on with new work. 'You will be glad to hear that within these last three weeks I have written 1000 lines – which are the third Book of my Poem,' he told Haydon. 'My Ideas with respect to it I assure you are very low – and I would write the subject thoroughly again. But I am tired of it and think the time would be better spent in writing a new Romance which I have in my eye for next summer – Rome was not built in a Day. and all the good I expect from my employment this summer is the fruit of Experience which I hope to gather in my next Poem.'

Meanwhile, Bailey was introducing him to new authors. Keats now began to read Milton, which, said Bailey, after 'the beauties of Spenser & the Faery Queen … gave his mind a mighty addition of energy & manly vigour.' In addition he read from Bailey's copies of Dante's *Inferno* translated into English, and William Hazlitt's philosophical work, *Principles of Human Action*. Bailey also shared Keats's profound admiration for Wordsworth, and they read and discussed his work constantly.

Afternoons were spent walking through the Oxfordshire countryside and boating on the Isis. 'Our conversation' remembered Bailey, 'rarely or never flagged, during our walks, or boatings, or in the evening.' As Keats came to know Bailey better his admiration grew; by the following January he was describing him

Oxford Sept 16th

My dear Fanny,

Let us now begin a regular question and answer - a little pro and con; letting it interfere as a pleasant method of my coming at your favourite little wants and enjoyments, that I may meet them in a way befitting a brother. We have been so little together since you have been able to reflect on things that I know not whether you prefer the History of King Pepin to Bunyan's Pilgrims Progress - or Cinderella and her glass slipper to Moore's Almanack. However in a few Letters I hope I shall be able to come at that and adapt my Scribblings to your Pleasure - You must tell me about all you read if it be only six Pages in a Week - and this transmitted to me every now and then will procure you full sheets of Writing from me pretty frequently - This this I feel as a necessity: for we ought to become intimately acquainted, in order that I may not only, as you grow up love you as my only Sister, but confide in you as my dearest friend. When I saw you last I told you of my intention of going to Oxford and 'tis now a Week since I disembark'd from his Whipship's Coach the Defiance in this place. I am living in Magdalen Hall on a visit to a young Man with whom I have not been long acquainted, but whom I like very much - we lead very industrious lives he in general Studies and I in proceeding at a pretty good rate with a Poem which I hope you will see early in the next year - Perhaps you might like to know what I am writing about - I will tell you.

Many Years ago there was a young handsome Shepherd who fed his flocks on a Mountains Side called Latmus - he was a very contemplative sort of a Person and lived solitary among the hills and Plains little thinking - that such a beautiful Creature as the Moon was growing mad in Love with him - However so it was; and when as 'one of the noblest men alive at the present day.' At the beginning of October they went to Stratford-on-Avon, going to Shakespeare's birthplace and to the church, where they signed the visitors book.

Three days later Keats returned to London. His brothers had returned from France, and he looked forward to seeing his friends. But to his dismay he found that everyone was bickering. 'Every Body seems at Loggerheads', he wrote to Bailey, 'There's Hunt infatuated – there's Haydon's Picture in statu quo. There's Hunt walks up and down his painting room criticising every head most unmercifully – There's Horace Smith tired of Hunt. "The web of our Life is of mingled Yarn."' It all contrasted badly with the quiet, studious life he had just been enjoying at Oxford; 'I am quite disgusted with literary men,' he told Bailey, 'and will never know another except Wordsworth.' A year ago he had been a willing disciple. Now, as he began to find his own voice as a poet, he needed independence. Shelley, then visiting Hunt, invited Keats to stay with him in Marlow, but he declined: 'I refused to visit Shelley,' he explained to Bailey, 'that I might have my own unfettered scope.'

Over the next few weeks he worked doggedly at the fourth and final book of *Endymion*. In November he went alone to Burford Bridge, near Boxhill in Surrey. His intention, he told Bailey, was 'to change the Scene – change the Air and give me a spur to wind up my Poem, of which there are wanting 500 lines.' Seven months earlier he had gone to the Isle of Wight to begin *Endymion*. Now, as he put the finishing touches to the poem, he was in a very different mood. Whereas before he had been unsure of his future as a poet, he was now full of confidence. *Endymion* was, he knew, imperfect, but he had a clear idea of where he was to go next. While at Burford Bridge he wrote a fine, philosophical letter to Bailey. 'Men of Genius' he said, 'are great as certain ethereal Chemicals operating on the Mass of neutral intellect – but they have not any individuality, any determined Character.' As a poet, he would draw back from 'the World's Quarrels', and trust in 'the authenticity of the imagination':

I am certain of nothing but of the holiness of the Heart's affections and the truth of Imagination – What the imagination seizes as Beauty must be truth – whether it existed before or not … The Imagination may be compared to Adam's dream – he awoke and found it truth.

What mattered, he told Bailey, was not his own happiness, but his truthful identification with external things: 'I scarcely remember counting on any Happiness – I look for it if it be not in the present hour – nothing startles me beyond the Moment. The setting sun will always set me to rights – or if a Sparrow come before my Window I take part in its existince and pick about the gravel.'

For six days Keats sat in his room and worked on the final lines of *Endymion*. On Friday, 28 November, he finished the poem.

⤳ *London: 1817–18*

K eats stayed on at Burford Bridge for another week, then returned to Well Walk at the beginning of December. After the long periods of solitude writing *Endymion* he now began to participate fully in London life. It was a lively world of dinners, theatre going, practical jokes and robust, sometimes bawdy humour, and Keats, with his exuberant, fun loving and convivial nature, enjoyed it to the full. Supportive and tolerant, he had a genius for friendship; 'Men should bear with each other,' he said, 'there lives not the Man who may not be cut up, aye hashed to pieces on his weakest side.'

Wentworth Place was a favourite destination, and a fast friendship grew between Keats and Dilke's neighbour, Charles Brown. A stout, worldly bachelor, Brown had spent five years as a merchant in St Petersburg. Shortly after his return to London he had received an inheritance that allowed him to live, as he termed it, a life of literary pursuits. He was to become perhaps Keats's most intimate friend. 'Keats never had a more zealous, a firmer, or more practical friend and advisor than Armitage Brown', Cowden Clarke later wrote.

Brown was the author of a comic opera, *Narensky*; or, *The Road to Yaroslaf*, which in 1814 had been produced at Drury Lane. The work was of negligible literary merit, but it did earn Brown a silver ticket giving him free lifetime entry to that theatre, and he and Keats became dedicated theatre-goers. One actor was then dominating the London stage – Edmund Kean. In the last few years Kean had revolutionised acting. His style was characterized by its intensity and passion, and to theatre-goers more accustomed to the calm, ceremonial dignity of earlier actors like Kemble, his small, dynamic figure and piercing voice were a revelation. Watching Kean act, said the poet Samuel Taylor Coleridge, was 'like reading Shakespeare by flashes of lightning.' Keats particularly admired the way Kean seemed to take on the very identity of the part he was playing. On 21 December he reviewed Kean's performance as Richard III in the *Champion*: 'There is an indescribable gusto in his voice,' he wrote, 'by which we feel that the utterer is thinking of the past and the future, while speaking of the instant … Other actors are continually thinking of their sum-total effect throughout a play. Kean delivers

himself up to the instant feeling, without a shadow of a thought about any thing else. He feels his being as deeply as Wordsworth, or any other of our intellectual monopolists.'

Wordsworth was currently in London. Keats now recognised him as by far the greatest of contemporary poets, and was tremendously excited by the prospect of

meeting him. The elder poet would have had some awareness of his young admirer; Haydon had, as promised, sent the 'Great spirits' sonnet to him, and Keats had sent him a copy his 1817 *Poems* inscribed 'with the author's sincere reverence.' They now met, towards the end of December, at the home of Wordsworth's cousin Thomas Monkhouse. Keats recited the 'Hymn to Pan' from Book One of *Endymion*, in response to which, according to Haydon, 'Wordsworth drily said, "a Very pretty piece of Paganism".' Haydon maintained that Keats 'never forgave' Wordsworth for this remark, but this seems unlikely, as the two poets met on half a dozen other occasions that winter. Wordsworth was, however, in a difficult mood at that time, and not generally approachable to those he did not know. In January the following year Keats was kept waiting at his lodgings, and was surprised when Wordsworth finally appeared in formal clothes, and clearly on his way out. A few days later, Keats dined with the Wordsworths, and started to argue a point; 'Mr Wordsworth is never interrupted,' said Wordsworth's wife Mary, putting a hand on his arm. But despite his disappointment at Wordsworth's character, Keats maintained his high opinion of his work – 'I am sorry that Wordsworth has left a bad impression wherever he visited in Town by his egotism, Vanity and bigotry', he wrote to his brothers in February, after Wordsworth had left London for the north, 'yet he is a great Poet if not a philosopher.'

One particularly memorable event took place that winter, an evening that has now come to be known as the 'Immortal Dinner.' The date was 28 December, and the host was Haydon. The guest list included Keats, Wordsworth, Charles Lamb, Thomas Monkhouse, the engraver John Landseer, and the explorer Joseph Ritchie. After dinner they sat before the vast unfinished canvas of Haydon's *Christ's Triumphal Entry into Jerusalem*, which now included, as members of the crowd, portraits of Wordsworth, Keats, the French writer Voltaire and the great scientist Isaac Newton. Wordsworth appeared to be in a good mood, Lamb, as was his habit, quickly became the worse for drink, and the proceedings grew lively. Haydon wrote in his diary:

> *Lamb got excessively merry and witty, and his fun in the intervals of Wordsworth's deep & solemn intonations of oratory was the fun & wit of the fool in the intervals of Lear's passion. Lamb soon gets tipsey, and tipsey he got*

very shortly, to our infinite amusement. "Now, you rascally Lake Poet," said Lamb, "you call Voltaire a dull fellow." We all agreed there was a state of mind when he would appear so– and "Well let us drink his health," said Lamb. "Here's Voltaire, the Messiah of the French nation, & a very fit one." He then attacked me for putting in Newton, "a Fellow who believed nothing unless it was as clear as the three sides of a triangle." And then he & Keats agreed that he had destroyed all the Poetry of the rainbow, by reducing it to a prism. It was impossible to resist them, and we drank "Newton's health, and confusion to mathematics!" It was delightful to see the good Humour of Wordsworth in giving in to all our frolics without affectation and laughing as heartily as the best of us.

Then, into this rather drunken scene walked John Kingston, Deputy Controller of Stamps. Haydon continues:

The Comptroller was a very mild & nice fellow but rather weak & very fond of talking. He got into conversation with Wordsworth on Poetry, and just after he had been putting forth some of his silly stuff, Lamb, who had been dozing as usual, suddenly opened his mouth and said, "What did you say, Sir?" "Why, Sir," said the Comptroller, in his milk & water insipidity, "I was saying &c., &c., &c." "Do you say so, Sir?" "Yes, Sir" was the reply. "Why then, Sir, I say, hiccup, you are – you are a silly fellow." This operated like thunder! The Comptroller knew nothing of his previous tipsiness & looked at him like a man bewildered.

While Wordsworth attempted to pacify Kingston, Haydon, Keats and Ritchie struggled to supress their laughter, as, undeterred, Lamb continued in the same vein:

The Comptroller went on making his profound remarks, and when anything very deep came forth, Lamb roared out,

> *Diddle iddle don*
> *My son John*

Went to bed with his breeches on

One stocking off & one stocking on,

My son John.

The Comptroller laughed as if he marked it, & went on; every remark Lamb chorused with

Went to bed with his breeches on

Diddle iddle on.

One person missing from the occasion was the writer William Hazlitt. A friend of Haydon's, Hazlitt was also present as a member of the crowd in *Christ's*

The essayist William Hazlitt by William Bewick. Keats greatly admired his 'depth of taste'.

Wordsworth Trust, Grasmere

Christ's Entry into
Jerusalem *by Haydon
(1820).*

St Mary's Seminary, Ohio

Entry into Jerusalem. Keats had first met him at Haydon's studio in 1816, and the critic had since come to have an increasingly important influence on his ideas. He owned copies of Hazlitt's books *The Principles of Human Action* and *Characters from Shakespeare's Plays*, both of which expounded the idea, recently formulated by Keats, of the poet as a passive agent acquiring the identities of others. In the new year Hazlitt began a series of lectures on the English poets. Keats missed the first lecture,

on Chaucer and Spenser, but over subsequent weeks he attended regularly. By now Hazlitt had replaced Hunt as, with Haydon and Wordsworth, one of his three 'great spirits'; on 10 January he wrote to Haydon: 'I am convinced that there are three things to rejoice at in this Age – The Excursion Your Pictures, and Hazlitt's depth of Taste'; 'allow me to add sincerely a fourth to be proud of,' Haydon replied, *'John Keats' genius!'*

Keats's conception of poetry was maturing all the time. 'The excellence of every Art is its intensity,' he had written to his brothers in December, 'capable of making all disagreeables evaporate, from their being in close relationship with Beauty & Truth.' Walking with Dilke one day, he had taken these ideas further:

> *several things dovetailed in my mind, & at once it struck me, what quality went to form a Man of Achievement especially in Literature & which Shakespeare possessed so enormously – I mean* Negative Capability, *that is when a man is capable of being in uncertainties, Mysteries, doubts, without any irritable reaching after fact & reason -*

Holding him back, however, was the job of preparing *Endymion* for the press. Between January and March Keats revised and copied the poem for publication, and found it a tedious task. 'I am anxious to get Endymion printed that I may forget it and proceed,' he told Taylor. He was planning a new poem, 'Hyperion', which would like *Endymion* be based on a Greek legend: the struggle between the Titans and the new generation of gods, the Olympians, and in particular the overthrow of Hyperion by Apollo, god of the sun and poetry. But where the earlier work was a loose romance, this was to be a more classical and tightly structured work; 'in Endymion I think you may have many bits of the deep and sentimental cast,' he told Haydon in January, 'the nature of Hyperion will lead me to treat it in a more naked and grecian Manner.' He was also planning to produce a volume jointly with Reynolds, to consist of poetic translations from Boccaccio's *Decameron*. He began with the tale of Isabella, and the murder of her lover Lorenzo by her two brothers.

Endymion was getting in the way of new work. But there was another distraction, and one far more disturbing. For some time, Keats's brother Tom had been showing worrying signs of ill health. Since December he had been living with George at Teignmouth on the south Devon coast where they hoped his condition might improve. On 6 March Keats joined them, and George returned to London the following day. He found his brother extremely ill. For some time he had convinced himself that Tom was not suffering from tuberculosis, the disease that had earlier claimed the life of their mother, but now the signs were unmistakeable. For the next six days the weather was appalling. Confined indoors, Keats listened to the rain against the window and brooded. On 13 March, Tom had a serious haemorrhage. 'I can hardly believe this melancholy news,' George wrote to Keats from London, 'Having so long accustomed myself to think altogether otherwise … Tom must never again presume on his strength, at all events untill he has *completely* recover'd.'

Deeply despondent, Keats sat down to write a preface for *Endymion*. 'In duty to the public I should have kept it back for a year or two, knowing it to be so faulty,' he wrote, 'but I really cannot do so: by repetition my favourite passages sound vapid in my ears, and I would rather redeem myself with a new Poem – should this one be found of any interest.' In April Reynolds wrote to Keats telling him that his publishers had rejected this impossible preface. 'Since you all agree that the thing is bad it must be so,' Keats replied, but he was unrepentant. A preface, he said, was addressed to the public, and he looked upon the public as an enemy: 'I have not the slightest feel of humility towards the Public,' he told Reynolds, 'or to anything in existence, – but the eternal Being, the principle of Beauty, – and the memory of great Men … I never write one single line of poetry, with the least shadow of public thought.' He did, however, make substantial revisions, and sent a modified version to London: 'I had an idea of giving no Preface' he wrote to Reynolds in an accompanying letter, 'however, don't you think this had better go? – O, let it – one should not be too timid – of committing faults.' Later that month *Endymion* was finally published.

Endymion *was published by Taylor and Hessey in 1818. The opening has become one of Keats's best-known lines.*

The British Library, London C39 f.31

ENDYMION.

BOOK I.

A THING of beauty is a joy for ever:
Its loveliness increases; it will never
Pass into nothingness; but still will keep
A bower quiet for us, and a sleep
Full of sweet dreams, and health, and quiet breathing.
Therefore, on every morrow, are we wreathing
A flowery band to bind us to the earth,
Spite of despondence, of the inhuman dearth
Of noble natures, of the gloomy days,
Of all the unhealthy and o'er-darkened ways   10

Despite everything Keats managed to continue with 'Isabella' at Teignmouth. He also planned a walking tour with Charles Brown through northern England and Scotland. 'I purpose within a Month to put my knapsack at my back and make a pedestrian tour through the North of England, and part of Scotland,' he told Haydon, 'to make a sort of Prologue to the Life I intend to pursue – that is to write, to study and to see all Europe at the lowest expence. I will clamber through the Clouds and exist.'

In the first week of May Keats left Teignmouth with Tom and returned to London. There he was faced with another worry. His brother George, who had never managed to settle into a career, had devised a scheme to emigrate to America, where he intended to buy some land. He had also become engaged to Georgiana Wylie, a warm-hearted nineteen year-old living with her widowed mother at Westminster. Suddenly Keats was faced with the prospect of losing both his brothers, one to illness and one to distance. 'I am in that temper that if I were under water I would scarcely kick to come to the top,' he wrote to Bailey on 25 May. 'I feel no spur at my brothers going to America and am almost stony-hearted about his wedding.' Ever the since the deaths of their parents, Keats, George and Tom had been extremely close. At Enfield, Cowden Clarke had noticed how Keats had shown 'an intensely tender affection for his brothers.' At Guy's Hospital, Henry Stephens had remarked that Keats's brothers 'worshipped him.' Now Keats explained to Bailey: 'My Love for my Brothers from the early loss of our parents and even for earlier Misfortunes has grown into an affection "passing the love of Women" – I have been ill temper'd with them, I have vex'd them – but the thought of them has always stifled the impression that any woman might otherwise have made upon me.' But he was fond of his future sister-in-law: 'I like her better and better,' he said, 'she is the most disinterrested woman I ever knew.' 'Disinterested' was one of Keats's highest expressions of praise – he defined it as 'a pure desire for the benefit of others'.

A few days later George and Georgiana were married. The following month, on 22 June, Keats, Brown, George and Georgiana left for Liverpool. From there George and Georgiana were to sail for America, and Keats and Brown were to travel north to begin their walking tour. Tom remained at Well Walk in the care of their landlord's wife, Mrs. Bentley. They arrived at Liverpool the next day, and early the following morning, while George and Georgiana were still sleeping, Keats and Brown left the inn and boarded a coach for Lancaster.

⤳ *Northern Tour: 1818*

At seven o'clock in the morning on 24 June, Keats and Brown left Lancaster in mist. 'There go a couple of gentlemen!' remarked a labourer, 'having nothing to do, they are finding out hard work for themselves!' It rained all day, but they made steady progress, reaching Endmoor, a village close to the southern tip of the Lake District, that evening. On the second day they had their first sight of the lakes and hills. For Keats it was a landscape on an entirely new scale; 'I cannot describe them,' he wrote to Tom, 'they surpass my expectation – beautiful water – shores and islands green to the marge – mountains all round up to the clouds.' They stopped for lunch at Bowness, on the southern shore of Windermere, and sampled the local trout.

A view of Windermere by J.M.W. Turner (1821).

Bridgeman Art Library/ Abbot Hall, Kendal

Keats asked after Wordsworth, and was dismayed to learn from the waiter that the poet, once admired by the younger generation for his radicalism, was now out campaigning for the right-wing Tory party for the forthcoming election. 'What think you of that?' he asked Tom. 'Sad – sad – sad.' In the afternoon they walked along the eastern shore of Windermere to Ambleside; 'our road was a winding lane,' Keats told Tom, 'wooded on each side, and green overhead, full of foxgloves.' At Ambleside they stopped for the night, and Keats read Brown his newly-finished poem, 'Isabella, or the Pot of Basil.' The following day they planned to see Wordsworth, who lived only two miles away at Rydal.

They rose the next morning at six, and before breakfast went to see Ambleside falls. They were small, but Keats had never seen anything like it: 'What astonishes me more than any thing is the tone, the coloring, the slate, the stone, the moss, the rock-weed; or, if I may so say, the intellect, the countenance of such places,' he told Tom. 'The space, the magnitude of mountains and waterfalls are well imagined before one sees them; but this countenance or intellectual tone must surpass every imagination and defy any remembrance. I shall learn poetry here and shall henceforth write more than ever, for the abstract endeavour of being able to add a mite to that mass of beauty which is harvested from these grand materials, by the finest spirits, and put into etherial existence for the relish of one's fellows. I cannot think with Hazlitt that these scenes make man appear little. I never forgot my stature so completely – I live in the eye; and my imagination, surpassed, is at rest.'

After breakfast they walked to Rydal. Just off the main road was Rydal Mount, Wordsworth's home, but to Keats's great disappointment neither the poet nor any member of his family were in. So, after leaving a note on the mantelpiece, they continued on the road north. After Rydal was the famous vale of Grasmere, and Keats noted those hills already known to him from Wordsworth's 'Poems on the Naming of Places': Loughrigg, Silver How, and Helm Crag. In the evening they came to Wythburn. After two days of constant walking Keats was not nearly as tired as he had expected: 'I have felt how much new Objects contribute to keep off a sense of Ennui and fatigue,' he wrote to George and Georgiana as he thought of their long journey to America. '14 Miles here is not so much as the 4 from Hampstead to London.'

The next morning they rose early. They had hoped to climb Helvellyn, England's second highest peak, but were prevented from doing so by mist, and so walked straight on to Keswick. Here, one of the most popular parts of the Lake District, they followed the conventional tourist route: a circuit of Derwentwater, visits to the falls of Lodore and the dramatic prehistoric stone circle at Castlerigg, and finally, the next morning, a guided ascent of Skiddaw, with its celebrated views of the Scottish coast, the Irish Sea, and most of the Lake District.

After climbing Skiddaw, Keats and Brown left the Lake District and continued north. They stopped at the Sun Inn in Ireby, an old market town, and were entranced by a children's dancing class being held upstairs: 'they kickit & jumpit with mettle extraordinary,' Keats wrote to Tom, '& whiskit, & fleckit, & toe'd it, & go'd it, & twirled it, & wheel'd it, & stampt it, & sweated it, tatooing the floor like mad. The difference between our country dances & these scotch figures, is about the same as leisurely stirring a cup o' Tea & beating up a batter pudding.' He was becoming used to the landscape, and was starting to notice the people. 'This is what I like better than scenery,' he told Tom, and now his travel letters really come to life. 'Scenery is fine – but human nature is finer' he had written to Bailey in March. 'The Sward is richer for the tread of a real, nervous, english foot – the eagles nest is finer for the Mountaineer has look'd into it.'

From Ireby they continued to Wigton and then on to Carlisle. The following day they entered Scotland, travelling by coach through Gretna Green to Dumfries. The great Scottish poet Robert Burns was buried in the churchyard here and Keats composed a sonnet, 'On visiting the tomb of Burns.' He was struck by the poverty of the local inhabitants; many of the children went bare-footed and most lived in wretched cottages, 'where smoke has no outlet but by the door.' For the next four days they followed the west coast of Scotland around through Dalbeattie, Kirkudbright and Glenluce to Stranraer. The country and the people gradually became more foreign: 'Our landlady of yesterday said very few Southrens passed these ways' wrote Keats from Auchencairn.

From Stranraer, they proceeded to Portpatrick. Here, they took a boat to Donagdhee in Ireland. It had been their intention to spend time in this country, but it proved to be far too expensive (three times that of Scotland) and they left after only

View from Skiddaw over Derwentwater (c.1777) by Thomas Hearne. Keats climbed Skiddaw in June 1818.

Bridgeman Art Library/ Yale Center for British Art

two days. They had been shocked by the apalling poverty, which was far worse than anything in Scotland. 'A Scotch cottage,' Keats remarked, 'though in that sometimes the smoke has no exit but at the door, is a pallace to an Irish one.' One terrible sight struck him particularly – 'The Duchess of Dunghill':

> *Imagine the worst dog kennel you ever saw placed upon two poles from a mouldy fencing – In such a wretched thing sat a squalid old Woman squat like an ape half starved from a scarcity of biscuit in its passage from Madagascar to the cape, – with a pipe in her mouth and looking out with a round-eyed skinny lidded, inanity – with a sort of horizontal idiotic movement of her head – squat and lean she sat and puff'd out smoke while two ragged tattered girls carried her along – what a thing would be a history of her life and sensations.*

Back in Portpatrick, they continued up the coast towards Ayr. By now they had become hardened walkers, and were achieving on average twenty miles a day. Keats began to look forward to seeing Burns's cottage at Alloway; 'One of the pleasantest means of annulling self is approaching such a shrine as the Cottage of Burns', he wrote to Reynolds, 'we need not think of his misery – that is all gone – bad luck to it – I shall look upon it hereafter with unmixed pleasure as I do upon my Stratford on Avon day with Bailey.' On 10 July they caught sight of Aisla Rock, a thousand foot granite island some way out to sea; 'Aisla struck me very suddenly,' Keats told Tom, 'really I was a little alarmed.' He composed a sonnet, 'To Aisla Rock', 'the only Sonnet of any worth I have of late written' he said. The following day they reached Burns's birthplace, and drank whisky with an old man who had known Burns and who bored them with endless anecdotes. Keats composed another sonnet, but this time found it so bad that he could not bring himself to transcribe it in his letters home.

On 13 July Keats and Brown entered Glasgow, 'under the most oppressive stare a body could feel' Keats told Tom. 'When we had crossed the Bridge Brown look'd back and said its whole population had turned to wonder at us.' They certainly made a curious sight, and on their journey through Scotland were variously mistaken for travelling jewellers, razor sellers, and, because Brown wore glasses, spectacle salesmen. 'Mr Abbey says we are Don Quixotes,' Keats wrote to his sister Fanny, 'tell

A letter from Keats to his brother Tom, 10–14 July 1818, one of several travel letters Keats wrote to him while walking through the north of Britain.

The British Library, London
Add. MS 45510 f.1v

To Ailsa Rock.

Hearken thou craggy ocean pyramid,
  Give answer by thy voice the Sea fowls screams
When were thy shoulders mantled in huge streams?
When from the Sun was thy broad forehead hid?
How long is't since the mighty Power bid
  Thee heave to airy sleep from fathom dreams—
Sleep in the Lap of Thunder or Sunbeams,
Or when grey clouds are thy cold Coverlid.
Thou answer'st not, for thou art dead asleep
  Thy Life is but two dead eternities
The last in Air, the former in the deep—
  First with the Whales, last with the eagle skies—
Drown'd wast thou till an Earthquake made thee steep
  Another cannot wake thy giant Size!—

"profanum vulgus" I must incline to the scotch. They never laugh, but they are always comparatively neat and clean. Their constitutions are not so remote and puzzling as the irish. The Scotchman will never give a decision on any point. he will never commit himself in a sentence which may be referred to as a meridian in his notion of things—so that you do not know him—and yet you may come in nigher neighbourhood to him than to the irishman who commits himself in so many places that it dizes your head. A Scotchman's motive is more easily discovered than an irishman's. a scotchman will go wisely about to deceive you, an irishman cunningly—An Irishman would bluster out of any discovery to his disadvantage—an Scotchman would retire perhaps without much desire of revenge. An Irishman likes to be thought a gallous fellow. A scotchman is contented with himself—It seems to me they are both sensible of the Character they hold in England and act accordingly to Englishmen. Thus the Scotchman will become over grave and over decent and the Irishman over-impetuous. I like a Scotchman best because he is less of a bore—I like the Irishman best because he ought to be more comfortable—The Scotchman has made up his Mind within himself in a sort of snail shell wisdom—The Irishman is full of strong headed instinct—The Scotchman is farther in Humanity than the Irishman—there his will stick perhaps when the Irishman shall be refined beyond him—for the former thinks he cannot be improved the latter would grasp at it for ever, place but the good plain before him. Maybole—Since breakfast we have come only four Miles to dinner, not merely for, we have examined in the way two fine old ruins called Crosragwell Abbey

this is the only sonnet of any worth I have of late written—I hope you will like it. 'T is now the 11th of July and we have come 8 Miles to Breakfast to Kirkoswald—I hope the next Kirk will be Kirk Alloway—I have nothing of consequence to say now concerning our journey—so I will speak as far as I can judge on the irish and scotch—I know nothing of the higher Classes yet I have a persuasion that there the Irish are victorious. As to the him we are more generally taken for pedlars.' In Glasgow Keats was approached by a drunkard: 'I put him off with my Arm – he returned all up in Arms saying aloud that, "he had seen all foreigners bu-u-u-t he never saw the like o' me" – I was obliged to mention the word Officer and Police before he would desist.'

Leaving Glasgow, they walked up the western shore of Loch Lomond towards Inverary. The scenery was beautiful, but the area was a bit too popular for their taste; the pleasure steamers and carriages of tourists, wrote Keats, 'take a little from the Pleasure of such romantic chaps as Brown and I.' On 17 July they walked around the northern end of Loch Fyne to Inverary where they heard a band playing at the Duke of Argyll's castle; 'I must say I enjoyed two or three common tunes,' Keats told Tom, 'but nothing could stifle the horrors of a solo on the Bag-pipe – I thought the Beast would never have done.'

Over the next few days Keats and Brown trudged on to Oban. Brown's feet began to suffer badly from new shoes, and the staple diet of eggs and oatcakes became extremely tedious. The people now spoke mostly Gaelic; 'I am for the first time in a country where a foreign Language is spoken,' wrote Keats, 'they gabble away in Gaelic at a vast rate.' On 21 July, after a fifteen mile walk in the pouring rain, they reached Oban. Here, after some debate about the expense involved, they decided to take a detour to the neighbouring islands of Mull, Staffa and Iona. It was to prove a fascinating, but physically exhausting experience. First, Brown and Keats took the ferry to the small island of Kerrera; this they walked across, and then travelled by boat to Mull. Then came a rugged thirty-seven mile walk with a guide across the island in appalling conditions. 'There's a wild place!' Brown later wrote to Dilke, 'Thirty seven miles of jumping and flinging over great stones along no path

'For solemnity and grandeur it far surpasses the finest Cathedral,' Keats wrote to his brother Tom of the hexagonal basalt pillars of Fingal's Cave, on the Scottish island of Staffa. Painting by William Daniell.

The Wordsworth Trust, Grasmere

at all, up the steep and down the steep and wading thro' rivulets up to the knees, and crossing a bog, a mile long, up to ancles.' In the middle of the island they spent the night at a shepherd's hut, and Keats resumed a letter to Bailey that he had begun at Inverary: 'I am more comfortable than I could have imagined in such a place, and so is Brown', he wrote. 'The People are all very kind.' As he sat, exhausted, in the humble, smoke-filled cottage, he examined his motives for taking the tour:

I should not have consented to myself these four Months tramping in the highlands but that I thought it would give me more experience, rub off more prejudice, use me to hardship, identify finer scenes load me with grander Mountains and strengthen more my reach in Poetry, than would stopping at home among books even though I should reach for Homer.

He was preparing himself for 'Hyperion', and his epic intentions were reflected in his reading; the only books he had taken with him, he told Bailey, were the three miniature volumes of Carey's translation of Dante's *Inferno*.

Having crossed Mull, Keats and Brown went by boat to the island of Iona, which for centuries had housed a monastery – 'Who would expect to find the ruins of a fine Cathedral Church, of Cloisters, Colleges, Monasteries and Nunneries in so remote an Island?' Keats wrote to Tom. From Iona they sailed to Staffa, and saw Fingal's Cave, an extraordinary natural cavern hollowed out by the sea and formed by basalt pillars. 'For solemnity and grandeur it far surpasses the finest Cathedrall,' wrote Keats, 'it is impossible to describe it.'

Back in Oban, Keats and Brown decided to rest for a few days before continuing north into the Highlands. Keats was suffering from a bad throat that was to trouble him for the rest of the trip, and for the first time his thoughts turned to home – 'I assure you I often long for a seat and a Cup o' tea at Well Walk,' he wrote to Tom, 'especially now that mountains, castles and Lakes are becoming common to me.'

After several days in Oban they set out again. Hampered by bad weather, fatigue, and Keats's worsening sore throat their progress was slow, but by the beginning of August they had reached Fort William, a little over fifty miles from

Oban. Here they intended to make one final effort and ascend Ben Nevis, which at nearly four and a half thousand feet was Britain's highest peak. At five o'clock the next morning they set out with a guide. For the first part of the stony ascent the weather was relatively good, but the last part of the journey was made in heavy mist. The going was rough: 'sometimes on two sometimes on three, sometimes four legs, ringing changes on foot, hand, stick, jump boggle, stumble, foot, hand, foot, (very gingerly) stick again, and then again a game at all fours.' On the summit Keats climbed the cairn, thereby getting 'a little higher than old Ben himself,' drank some whisky, and wrote a sonnet, before making, as he put it, a 'most vile descent – shook me all to pieces.' 'I am heartily glad it is done,' Keats told Tom afterwards, 'it is almost like a fly crawling up a wainscot.'

Keats and Brown walked north for another four days, and on 6 August reached Inverness. Keats had hoped to carry on after a few days rest, but it quickly became evident that his sore throat would make this impossible, and so, reluctantly, he and Brown agreed to part. The following day, Keats took the coach to Cromarty, and from there the packet boat south to London.

Ben Nevis, Britain's highest peak.

The British Library, London 010370 e 41

~ *'Hyperion': 1818*

Keats arrived back in Hampstead on 18 August, and presented himself at Wentworth Place in his traveller's garb. 'John Keats arrived here last night as brown and as shabby as you can imagine,' wrote a surprised Mrs Dilke in her diary, 'scarcely any shoes left, his jacket all torn at the back, a fur cap, a great plaid, and his knapsack. I cannot tell what it looked like.' Keats was in high spirits, but the Dilkes had bad news. While he had been away Tom's health had deteriorated badly. He was now desperately ill with tuberculosis.

In September the reviews of *Endymion* came in. They were devastating. At the beginning of the month an attack on both *Poems* and *Endymion* was published in *Blackwoods Magazine*. Keats had been expecting this. For some weeks the magazine, under the pseudonym of 'Z' (the critics John Gibson Lockhart and John Wilson) had published a series of attacks on Leigh Hunt and his 'cockney school of poetry.' They despised Hunt not only for his liberal politics, but for his easy style, pretty imagery and lazy use of myth. Keats had of course developed since his early admiration of Hunt, but in the public's eye the two men were still closely linked. Hunt had introduced Keats to the public in the *Examiner*, while Keats's 1817 *Poems* had been dedicated to Hunt, and many of the poems in that volume betrayed Hunt's influence. It was inevitable that Lockhart and Wilson would sooner or later turn their sights on Keats, and now they did so with extraordinary savagery. 'Mr Hunt is a small poet but he is a clever man', they wrote, 'Mr Keats is a still smaller poet, and he is only a boy

Keats went immediately to Well Walk. Eight years before he had nursed his mother through the last, terrible stages of the disease; now he sat up day and night with his youngest brother. It was an exhausting task, and a solitary one. George was in America, and young Fanny, still under Abbey's guardianship, was only allowed to make a few visits. Isolated, and still troubled by the sore throat caught in Scotland, Keats found himself being drawn into Tom's illness; 'I wish I could say Tom was any better,' he wrote to Dilke. 'His identity presses upon me so all day that I am obliged to go out – and although I intended to have given some time to study alone I am obliged to write, and plunge into abstract images to ease myself of his countenance his voice and feebleness – so that I live now in a continual fever.'

Opposite page:

A posthumous portrait of Keats by William Hilton, adapted from Severn's miniature on page 8.

National Portrait Gallery, London

of pretty abilities, which he has done everything in his power to spoil.' Earlier that year Lockhart had met Benjamin Bailey at a dinner in Scotland, and while attempting to defend his friend, Bailey had revealed details about Keats's early life as a medical apprentice. The reviewers now used this information to fuel their attack:

> *His friends, we understand, destined him to the career of medicine, and he was bound apprentice some years ago to a worthy apothecary in town. But all has been undone by a sudden attack of the malady to which we have alluded. . . . It is a better and a wiser thing to be a starved apothecary than a starved poet; so back to the shop Mr John, back to 'plasters, pills, and ointment boxes,' &c. But, for Heaven's sake, young Sangrado, be a little more sparing of extenuatives and soporifics in your practice than you have been in your poetry*

Later in September a review of *Endymion* by John Wilson Croker was published in the *Quarterly Review*. Although Croker admitted that Keats had 'power of language, rays of fancy, and gleams of genius' he went on to condemn him as 'a copyist of Mr Hunt.' Furthermore, he was 'more unintelligible, almost as rugged, twice as diffuse, and ten times more tiresome and absurd than his prototype.' Croker confessed that he had been unable to get beyond the first book of the poem.

When Taylor read the reviews he was furious; 'it has been thought necessary,' he wrote to John Clare, 'in the leading Review, the Quarterly, to damn his [poetry] for imputed political Opinions – Damn them who could act in so cruel a way to a young man of undoubted Genius.' 'It was done in the Spirit of the Devil,' he wrote angrily to the editor of *Blackwoods*. Two weeks after the *Blackwoods* review Keats dined at Hessey's, and surprised everyone by threatening to give up writing. Hessey, however, could see that beneath his abrupt changes of mood there was a deep resolve:

> *He is studying closely, recovering his Latin, going to learn Greek, and seems altogether more rational than usual – but he is such a man of fits and starts he is not much to be depended on. Still he thinks of nothing but poetry as his being's end and aim, and sometime or other he will, I doubt not, do something valuable.*

Sure enough, several weeks later Keats was writing to Hessey in a spirit of renewed confidence:

The Genius of Poetry must work out its own salvation in a man: It cannot be matured by law & precept, but by sensation & watchfulness in itself – That which is creative must create itself – In Endymion, I leaped headlong into the Sea, and thereby have become better acquainted with the Soundings, the quicksands, & the rocks, than if I had stayed upon the green shore, and piped a silly pipe, and took tea & comfortable advice. – I was never afraid of failure; for I would sooner fail than not be among the greatest . . .

Endymion had served its purpose, and he had no illusions about its quality. He was clear-sighted in his ambitions for the future. 'Praise or blame has but a momentary effect on the man whose love of beauty in the abstract makes him a severe critic on his own Works,' he explained to Hessey. 'My own domestic criticism has given me pain without comparison beyond what Blackwood or the Quarterly could possibly inflict.' Reynolds published a defence of *Endymion* in *Alfred, West of England Journal*, and urged Keats to publish 'Isabella' as a reply to the reviewers, but Keats refused – the poem was not of sufficient quality. 'This is a mere matter of the moment,' he wrote with quiet confidence to George and Georgiana on 14 October 1818. 'I think I shall be among the English Poets after my death.'

Someone, however, had been thoroughly alarmed by Keats's threat to give up poetry. This was Richard Woodhouse, Taylor and Hessey's legal advisor, and a devoted friend and supporter of Keats. In October Keats wrote to Woodhouse to assure him that such 'fits and starts' as Hessey termed them, were not just an aspect of his personality, but were intrinsic to the poetic character:

As to the poetical Character itself, (I mean that sort of which, if I am any thing, I am a Member; that sort distinguished from the wordsworthian or egotistical sublime; which is a thing per se and stands alone) it is not itself – it has no self – it is every thing and nothing – It has no character – it enjoys light and shade; it lives in gusto, be it foul or fair, high or low, rich or, mean or

71

elevated – It has as much delight in conceiving an Iago as an Imogen. What shocks the virtuous philosopher delights the camelion Poet.

With such a character, Keats asked Woodhouse, 'where is the Wonder that I should say I would write no more? ... It is a wretched thing to confess; but is a very fact that not one word I ever utter can be taken for granted as an opinion growing out of my identical nature – how can it, when I have no nature?' There was a more personal reason for his shifting attitudes. Sociable as he was, Keats always maintained a certain detachment – the innermost part of his nature remained hidden. 'They do not know me not even my most intimate acquaintance,' he wrote to George, 'I give into their feelings as though I were refraining from irritating a little child ... because I have in my own breast so great a resource.'

That autumn Keats began the long-planned 'Hyperion', and from the opening lines the poetry has a weight and assurance that is quite new. The scene introduces Saturn, shortly after the Titans have been overthrown by the new gods:

> *Deep in the shady sadness of a vale*
> *Far sunken from the healthy breath of morn,*
> *Far from the fiery noon, and eve's one star,*
> *Still as the silence round about his lair;*
> *Forest on forest hung above his head*
> *Like cloud on cloud. No stir of air was there,*
> *Not so much as on a summer's day*
> *Robs not one light seed from the feathered grass,*
> *But where the dead leaf fell there did it rest.*
> *The stream went voiceless by, still deadened more*
> *By reason of his fallen divinity*
> *Spreading a shade: the Naiad 'mid her reeds*
> *Press'd her cold finger closer to her lips.*

The controlled, austere rhythm of the blank verse is in the strongest possible contrast to the loose couplets of *Endymion*.

The original
manuscript of
'Hyperion' (1818),
Keats's second attempt
at an epic poem.

The British Library,
London
Add. MS 37000 f.1

Hyperion Book 1st

Deep in the shady sadness of a Vale,
Far sunken from the healthy breath of Morn,
Far from the fiery noon, and ~~evening~~ Eve's one star,
Sat grey hair'd Saturn quiet as a Stone,
Stile as the silence round about his Lair.
Forest on forest hung above his head
~~Like Clouds that whose brows thunderous bosoms~~
Like Cloud on Cloud. No stir of air was there;
~~Not so much life as ~~what~~ a young vulture~~
~~No ~~spread upon a field of green said corn:~~
But where the dead leaf fell, there did it rest.
A Stream went voiceless by, still deadened more
By reason of his fallen divinity
~~The dieu adest ij~~
~~Spreading a~~ shade: the Naïad mid her reeds
Push'd her cold finger closer to her lips.

Along the margin sand large foot marks went
No further than to where his feet had stay'd so often
and slept ~~without there since~~ a motion: ~~since that time~~ ~~whoso the~~ ground
~~the~~ ~~resting~~
His old right hand lay nerveless ~~on the ground~~ listless, dead
Unsceptcid; and his ~~white broad realmless eyes were closd;~~
While his ~~bowed~~ head seem'd listening to the Earth
~~The~~ His ancient Mother for some comfort yet.

Thus the old Eagle drowsy with ~~his grief great~~ ~~self~~
Sat moulting his weak Plumage never more
To be restored or soar against the Sun,
While his three Sons upon Olympus stood—

It seem'd no force could wake him from his place
But there came one, who, with a kindred hand
Touch'd his wide Shoulders, after bending low
With reverance, though to one who knew it not.
She was a Goddess of the infant world;
~~By her ~~ ~~the~~ tallest Amazon
Had stood a ~~little~~ ~~Pigm~~y's height: she would have ta'en
Achilles by the hair and bent his neck,
Or with a ~~finger~~ Ixion's toil

John Keats

Nursing Tom, and working steadily at 'Hyperion', Keats lived a confined life. But he still found time for diversion. In September he called on Reynolds's sisters, and there met their beautiful cousin, Jane Cox. 'When she comes into a room she makes an impression the same as the Beauty of a Leopardess,' he wrote to George. 'I always find myself more at ease with such a woman; the picture before me always gives me a life and animation which I cannot possibly feel with any thing inferiour – I am at such times too much occupied in admiring to be awkward or on a tremble. I forget myself entirely because I live in her. You will by this time think I am in love with her; so before I go any further I will tell you I am not – she kept me awake one Night as a tune of Mozart's might do.'

Then at the end of October he had a chance meeting on the street with Isabella Jones, the woman he had met some time ago in Hastings. He accompanied her back to her home in Bloomsbury. 'We went up to her sitting room,' he told George, 'a very tasty sort of place with Books, Pictures a bronze statue of Buonaparte, Music, aeolian harp … a case of choice Liquers &c. &c. … As I had warmed with her before and kissed her – I thought it would be living backwards not to do so again – she had a better taste: she perceived how much a thing of course it was and shrunk from it – not in a prudish way but in as I say good taste.' She asked him to keep her existence secret, and he agreed – he never once mentions her name in his letters.

Isabella Jones remained, Keats said, 'an enigma.' But at about this time he had a meeting of more lasting significance. While he and Brown were in Scotland, a family called Brawne had rented Brown's half of Wentworth Place, and on their return had moved to house nearby. Mrs Brawne was a widow. Her eldest daughter, Fanny, was eighteen years old, lively and entrancing. In time she would dominate Keats's emotional existence. At this point, however, he still saw the poetic life as solitary, and incompatible with marriage. He wrote to his newly-married brother:

Notwithstanding your Happiness and your recommendation I hope I shall never marry. Though the most beautiful Creature were waiting for me at the end of a Journey or a Walk; though the carpet were of Silk, the Curtains of the morning Clouds; the chairs and Sofa stuffed with Cygnet's down; the food Manna, the Wine beyond Claret, the Window opening of Winander mere, I should not feel – or rather my happiness would not be so fine, as my Solitude is sublime. Then instead of what I have described, there is a Sublimity to welcome me home. The roaring of the wind is my wife and the Stars through the window pane are my Children.

Keats's letter to his sister Fanny written on the morning of their brother Tom's death (30 November 1818).

The British Library, London
Add. MS 34019 f.15

At any rate, it was hardly a time for romance. That autumn and winter Tom's condition steadily worsened, and at the end of November he suffered a final relapse. On the morning of 30 November, Keats wrote to his sister: 'Poor Tom has been so bad that I delayed your visit hither – as it would be painful to you both. I cannot say he is any better this morning – he is in a very dangerous state – I have scarce any hopes of him – keep up your spirits for me my dear Fanny.' That same morning, at eight o'clock, Tom died. He was just nineteen years old. Brown, at Wentworth Place, was the first to hear the news: 'Early one morning I was awakened in my bed by a pressure on my hand. It was Keats, who came to tell me that his brother was no more.'

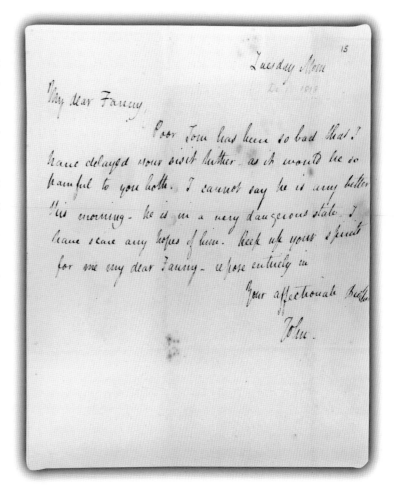

≈ *Wentworth Place: 1818–19*

Brown immediately suggested that Keats leave Well Walk, which would ever be associated with Tom, and come and live with him at Wentworth Place. Keats accepted, and over the next few weeks his friends distracted him with a relentless series of social events; he was taken to dinners, to the theatre, and even to the prize fight between Jack Rendall and Ned Turner, fought over thirty-four rounds at Sussex on 5 December. 'The last days of poor Tom were of the most distressing nature,' he wrote to George and Georgiana, 'but his last moments were not so painful, and his very last was without a pang – I will not enter into any parsonic comments on death – yet the common observations of the commonest people on death are as true as their proverbs. I have scarce a doubt of immortality of some nature or other – neither had Tom.'

Wentworth Place in Hampstead, as it is today. Now known as Keats House, it is open to the public.

Keats House, London

Over the next few weeks Keats gradually added to this letter – the first of a series of enormous packets he was to send to America in the coming year. Keats's letters have become justly famous, and are now as closely studied as his poems. Their range is enormous: everything is included, from the most profound philosophical reflections and revealing self-analysis to the most trivial gossip. No one thought harder or more frequently about poetry than Keats, and through the letters we can trace, month by month, his development as a poet. The long letters to George and Georgiana, in particular, are so frank and spontaneous that they read like a personal diary, and one can almost hear his conversational voice.

After his brief words on Tom's death, Keats went on to describe his new friend, Fanny Brawne:

> *[She] is I think beautiful and elegant, graceful, silly, fashionable and strange. We have a little tiff now and then ... she is not seventeen – but she is ignorant – monstrous in her behaviour flying out in all directions, calling people such names – that I was forced lately to make use of the term Minx – this is I think not from any innate vice but from a penchant she has for acting stylishly.*

Chichester Cathedral in a watercolour by John Constable (c.1834). Keats stayed at Chichester in January and February 1819.

Victoria & Albert Museum, London

77

Two days later, he told George and Georgiana that he was looking forward to a quieter period in which to resume his writing. Only poetry allowed him to express that essential part of himself which he habitually kept concealed in society:

I feel I must again begin with my poetry – for if I am not in action mind or Body I am in pain – and from that I suffer greatly by going into parties where from the rules of society and a natural pride I am obliged to smother my Spirit and look like an Idiot – because I feel my impulses given way to would too much amaze them – I live under an everlasting restraint – Never relieved except when I am composing – so I will write away.

He and Brown had received an invitation to stay with Dilke's mother and father at Chichester, but he was reluctant; 'look here', he told Woodhouse, 'I have a new leaf to turn over – I must work – I must read – I must write – I am unable to afford time for new acquaintances.' However he eventually agreed, and arrived in Chichester on the evening of 18 January 1819.

'You will find him a very odd young man,' Mrs Dilke had warned her parents-in-law before Keats's arrival, 'but good-tempered and very clever indeed.' She needn't have worried, however, for Keats got on well with his hosts. He and Brown happily joined the Dilkes' card playing circle, and the house itself was comfortable; from its upper floors it had a fine outlook over most of the city. Chichester, with its ancient walls, Norman cathedral and medieval architecture, evidently delighted him.

The relaxed, good-humoured company, the atmosphere of the city, and the desire to write, now inspired Keats to begin one of his most successful, and popular poems, 'The Eve of St Agnes'. In the poem Madeline retires from a great party to her room, hoping that, according to the legend of St Agnes, she will have visions of her future husband. That night Porphyro, her lover but an enemy of the family, steals into the house, and with help of her nurse, finds Madeline and escapes with her into a storm. Writing with confidence, Keats sustains the rhythm of this narrative brilliantly, and paints each scene with such richness and intricacy that the poem has a wonderfully immediate, physical feel:

Down the wide stairs a darkling way they found. -

In all the house was heard no human sound.

A chain-droop'd lamp was flickering by each door;

The arras, rich with horsemen, hawk, and hound,

Flutter'd in the besieging wind's uproar;

And the long carpets rose along the gusty floor.

They glide, like phantoms, into the wide hall;

Like phantoms, to the iron porch, they glide;

Where lay the porter in uneasy sprawl,

With a huge empty flaggon by his side:

The wakeful blood hound rose, and shook his hide,

But his sagacious eye an inmate owns:

By one, and one, the bolts full easy slide:-

The chains lie silent on the footworn stones;-

The key turns, and the door upon its hinges groans.

At the beginning of February Keats returned to Wentworth Place. He began another poem inspired by his stay in Chichester, 'The Eve of St Mark', though never finished it – 'I began a Poem call'd 'the Eve of St Mark' quite in the spirit of Town quietude', he later told George and Georgiana. 'I think it will give you the sensation of walking about an old country Town in a coolish evening.'

It had been an enjoyable and productive few weeks, but in February and March a depression fell over Keats. He did little, and wrote nothing. There was no news from George in America, and most of his friends seemed to be out of town. Haydon, as usual in deep financial crisis, was pestering him for money. On 14 February he wrote to George and Georgiana: 'I see very little now, and very few persons – being almost tired of men and things ... the Literary world I know nothing about.' On 3 March he wrote again: 'I look back upon the last month, and find nothing to write about, indeed, I do not recollect one thing particular in it.' The idea of a literary life now seemed to depress him, and he even toyed with idea of training as a physician in Edinburgh. To Haydon he wrote on 8 March: 'You must be

The Flight of
Madelaine and
Porphyro *(1848), by
William Holman Hunt.
When Hunt began this
painting, showing a
scene from 'The Eve of
St. Agnes', in 1846, he
believed it was the first
to be based upon the
work of that 'still little-
known poet', Keats.*

*Guildhall Library,
Corporation of London*

81

John Keats

*The manuscript of
'The Eve of St Mark',
the poem Keats began
shortly after leaving
Chichester in 1819.*

*The British Library,
London
Egerton MS 2780 f.33*

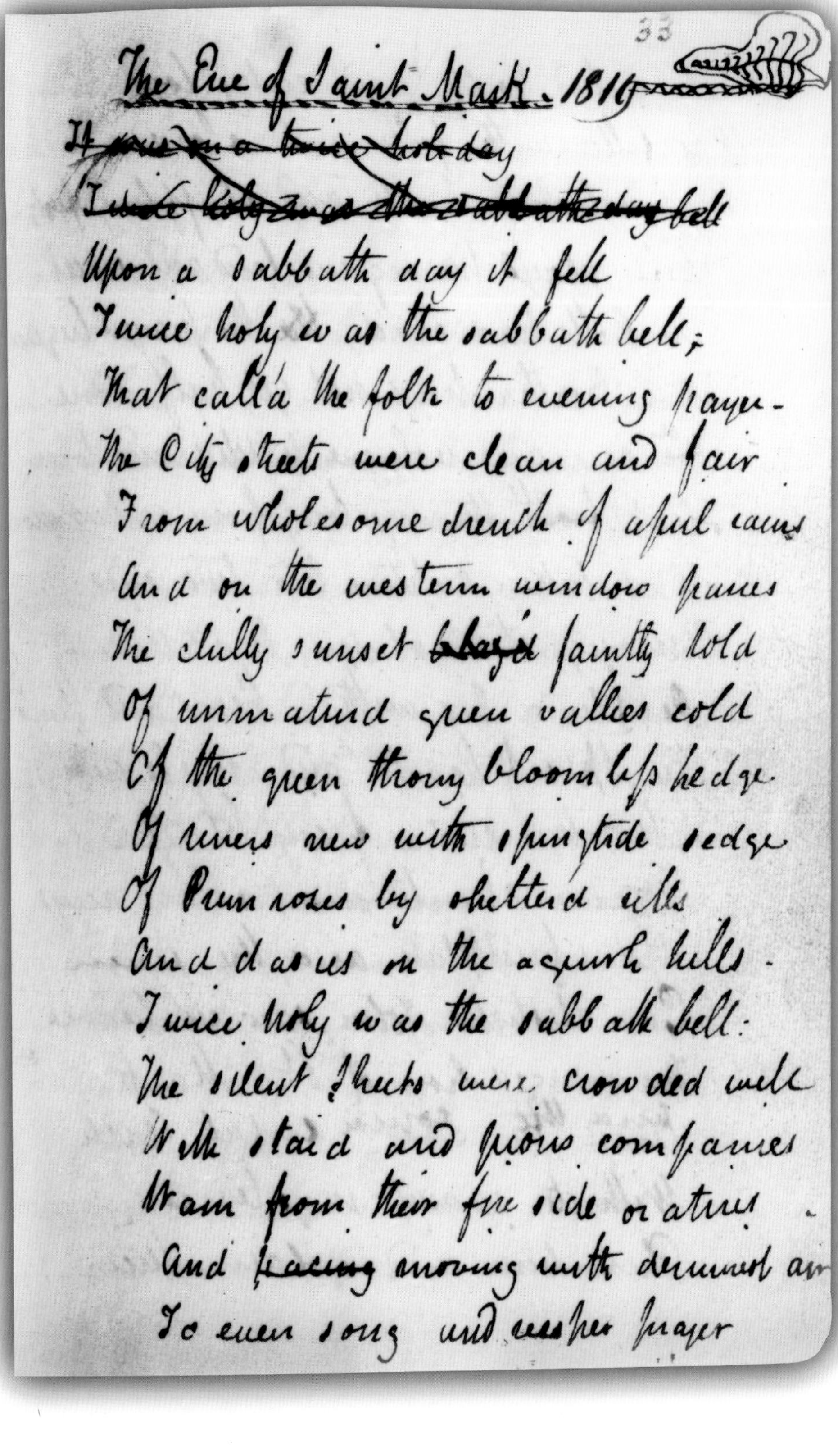

The Eve of Saint Mark. 1819

~~If you in a twice look day~~

~~Twice holy was the sabbath day bell~~

Upon a sabbath day it fell
Twice holy was the sabbath bell;
That call'd the folk to evening prayer—
The City streets were clean and fair
From wholesome drench of april rains
And on the western window panes
The chilly sunset ~~blazed~~ faintly told
Of unmatured green vallies cold
Of the green thorny bloomless hedge
Of rivers new with springtide sedge
Of Primroses by sheltered rills
And daisies on the aguish hills.
Twice holy was the sabbath bell:
The silent Streets were crowded well
With staid and pious companies
Warm from their fire side oratries
And moving with demurest air
To even song and vesper prayer

wondering where I am and what I am about! I am mostly at Hampstead, and about nothing ... I will not mix with that most vulgar of all worlds the literary ... I am three and twenty with little knowledge and middling intellect; It is true that in the height of enthusiasm I have been cheated into some fine passages but that is nothing.'

In April, however, his mood began to improve. That month Dilke left Wentworth Place to be nearer his son, now at boarding school in Westminster, and rented his half of the house to the Brawnes, who thus became Keats's neighbours. He and Fanny now began to grow more intimate. He gave her a copy of Dante's *Inferno*, and in the flyleaf Fanny copied out Keats's most famous sonnet, a poem with which she has always been closely associated:

> *Bright star! would I were steadfast as thou art –*
> *Not in lone splendour hung aloft the night*
> *And watching, with eternal lids apart,*
> *Like nature's patient, sleepless Eremite,*
> *The moving waters at their priestlike task*
> *Of pure ablution round earth's human shores,*
> *Or gazing on the new soft fallen mask*
> *Of snow upon the mountains and the moors –*
> *No – yet still steadfast, still unchangeable,*
> *Pillow'd on my fair love's ripening breast,*
> *To feel for ever its soft fall and swell,*
> *Awake for ever in a sweet unrest'*
> *Still, still to hear her tender-taken breath*
> *And so live ever – or else swoon to death.*

On 15 April, after a break of almost a month, Keats resumed his current letter to George and Georgiana. The last few days, he said, had been eventful. He had been to a party with Reynolds and met 'one of the most beautiful Girls I ever saw'; one night he had played cards with some friends at Wentworth Place until dawn; Reynolds had just written a brilliant parody of Wordsworth's *Peter Bell*; on Sunday, while walking on Hampstead Heath, he had met his old anatomy demonstrator at Guy's Hospital,

Bright Star, would I were stedfast as thou art —
Not in lone splendor hung aloft the night
And watching, with eternal lids apart,
Like natures patient, sleepless Eremite,
The moving waters at their priestlike task
Of pure ablution round earths human shores,
Or gazing on the new soft-fallen masque
Of snow upon the mountains and the moors.
No — yet still stedfast, still unchangeable
Pillow'd upon my fair love's ripening breast,
To feel for ever its soft swell and fall,
Awake for ever in a sweet unrest;
Still, still to hear her tender-taken breath,
And so live ever or else swoon to death.

The 'Bright Star' sonnet, written by Keats in his copy of The Poetical Works of William Shakespeare, *opposite the poem 'A Lover's Complaint'.*

Keats House, London

Joseph Green, with Samuel Taylor Coleridge, and for the next hour was an audience to one of Coleridge's famous monologues: 'In those two miles he broached a thousand things – let me see if I give you a list,' he wrote to George and Georgiana. 'Nightingales, Poetry – on Poetical sensation – Metaphysics – Different genera and species of Dreams – Nightmare – a dream accompanied by a sense of touch – single and double touch – A dream related – First and second consciousness – Monsters – the Kraken – Mermaids – Southey believes in them – Southey's belief too much diluted – A Ghost story – Good morning.'

The following day he told his brother and sister-in-law of an unpleasant discovery he had just made. He had gone to Well Walk to pick up Tom's remaining papers, and had found a packet of love letters, apparently from a mysterious French woman, Amena Bellefila, but in fact written by a friend of Tom's, Charles Wells. The deception roused Keats to uncharacteristic fury: 'He is a rat and he shall have ratsbane to his vanity,' he wrote of Wells. 'I will harm him all I possibly can.' Five days later he again took up the letter, and gave George and Georgiana a recent poem, 'La Belle Dame Sans Merci':

> *O what can ail thee knight at arms*
> *Alone and palely loitering*
> *The sedge has withered from the Lake*
> *And no birds sing!*
>
> *O what can ail thee knight at arms*
> *So haggard and so woe begone?*
> *The squirrel's granary is full*
> *And the harvest's done.*

This masterly poem, which continues for another ten stanzas, appears to come out of nowhere. It is now one of Keats's best known poems, but he himself considered it a trifle. The letter then continues with one of his most impressive philosophical passages. 'Call the world if you Please "The vale of Soul-making,"' he wrote. 'Then you will find out the use of the world. I say "Soul making" Soul as distinguished from an Intelligence – There may be intelligences or sparks of the divinity in millions – but they are not Souls till they acquire identities, till each one is personally itself.' How, he asks, are these souls to be acquired? – 'How, but by the medium of a world like this?':

> *I will call the world a School instituted for teaching little children to read – I will call the human heart the horn Book used in that School – and I will call the Child able to read, the Soul made from that school and its hornbook. Do you not see how necessary a World of Pains and troubles is to school an Intelligence and make it a soul? A Place where the heart must feel and suffer in a thousand diverse ways!*

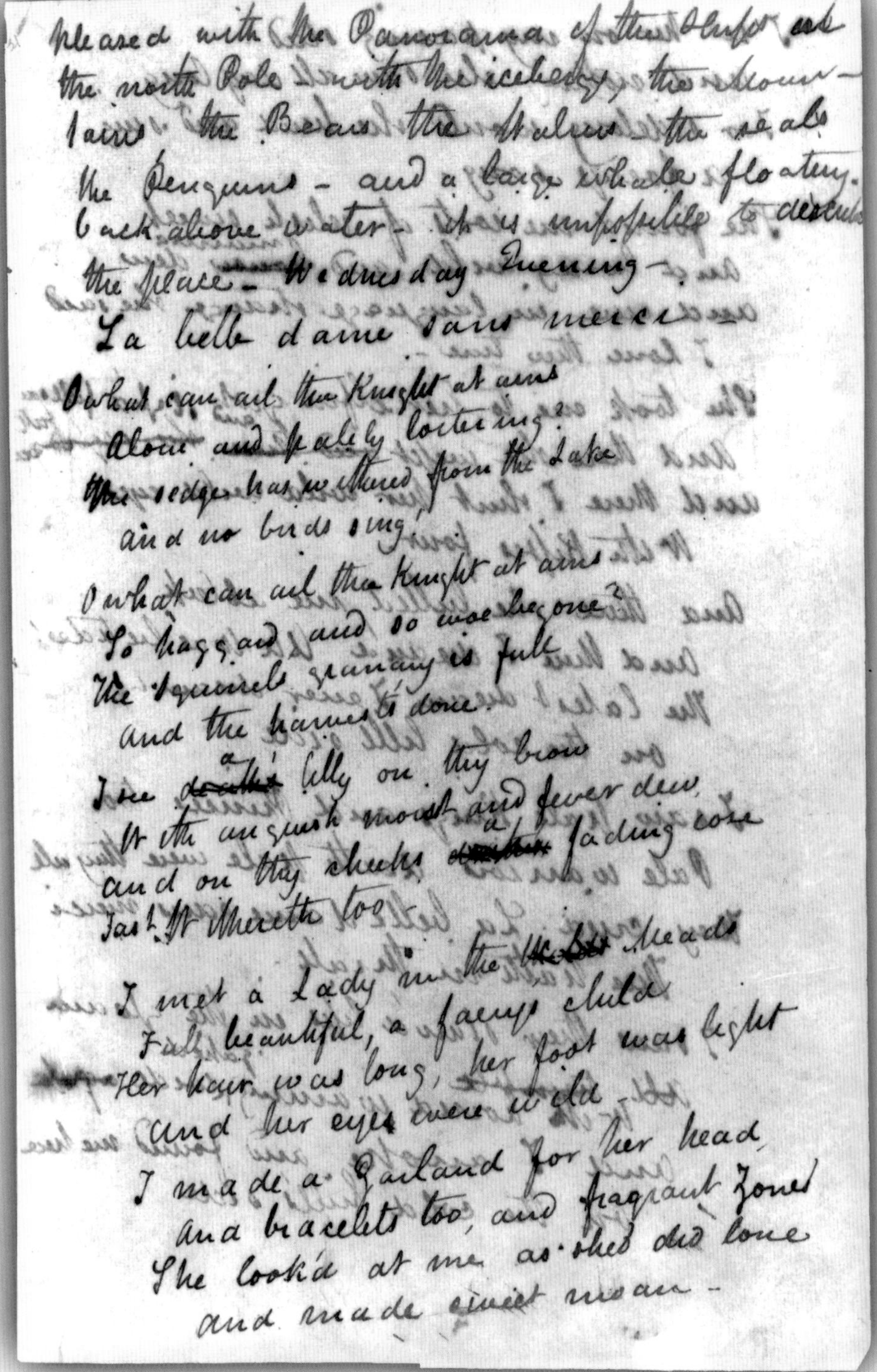

pleased with the Panorama of the ships at
the north Pole - with the icebergs, the Mountains the Bears the Walrus - the seals
the Penguins - and a large whale floating
back above water - it is impossible to describe
the place - Wednesday Evening -

La belle dame sans merci -

O what can ail thee Knight at arms
Alone and palely loitering?
The sedge has withered from the Lake
And no birds sing!

O what can ail thee knight at arms
So haggard and so woe begone?
The squirrel's granary is full
And the harvest's done.

I see ~~death's~~ a lilly on thy brow
With anguish moist and fever dew,
And on thy cheeks ~~death's~~ a fading rose
Fast Withereth too -

I met a Lady in the ~~Wilds~~ Meads
Full beautiful, a faery's child
Her hair was long, her foot was light
And her eyes were wild -

I made a Garland for her head,
And bracelets too, and fragrant Zone
She look'd at me as she did love
And made sweet moan -

Part of the lengthy letter Keats wrote to his brother and sister-in-law in America between 14 February and 3 May 1819, showing his great poem 'La Belle Dame sans Merci'.

The Houghton Library, Harvard University, Massachusetts

'There now,' wrote Keats, 'I think what with Poetry and Theology you may thank your Stars that my pen is not very long winded.' He now transcribed for George and Georgiana a few poems, including 'Ode to Psyche', which he introduced as: 'the first and only poem with which I have taken even moderate pains – I have for the most part dash'd off my lines in a hurry – This I have done leisurely – I think it reads the better for it and will encourage me to write other things in even a more peaceable and healthy spirit.' Finally, on 3 May, he brought the letter to a close. The weather he said, was fine: 'everything is in delightful forwardness; the violets are not withered, before the peeping of the first rose.'

That May, Keats wrote his great odes: 'Ode to a Nightingale', 'Ode on a Grecian Urn' and 'Ode on Melancholy.' The fine weather, the comfort and calm of life at Wentworth Place and its garden – he and Brown in one half of the house, the Brawnes in the other – allowed Keats to compose, as he had wished, in a 'peaceable and healthy spirit.' 'Ode to a Nightingale' was written, according to Brown, one morning under a plum-tree in the garden of Wentworth Place. The poem contrasts the world of human suffering and change with the ideal, unchanging world of nature:

> *My heart aches, and a drowsy numbness pains*
> *My sense, as though of hemlock I had drunk,*
> *Or emptied some dull opiate to the drains*
> *One minute past and Lethe-wards had sunk:*
> *'Tis not through envy of thy happy lot,*
> *But being too happy in thine happiness, -*
> *That thou, light-winged Dryad of the trees,*
> *In some melodious plot*
> *Of beechen green, and shadows numberless,*
> *Singest of summer in full-throated ease.*

The poetry has a personal immediacy absent from Keats's work until now; one section in particular recalls the recent death of Tom:

The weariness, the fever, and the fret

Here, where men sit and hear each other groan;

Where palsy shakes a few, sad, last gray hairs,

Where youth grows pale, and spectre-thin, and dies.

Where 'Ode to a Nightingale' contrasts human life with nature, 'Ode on a Grecian Urn', with its famous last line, contrasts it with the perfect world of classical art, as represented by the Grecian urn:

John Keats

A posthumous portrait of Keats listening to a nightingale, by Joseph Severn.

Keats House, London

O Attic shape! Fair attitude! with brede

Of marble men and maidens overwrought,

With forest branches and the trodden weed;

Thou, silent form, doth tease us out of thought

As doth eternity: Cold Pastoral!

When old age shall this generation waste,

Thou shalt remain, in midst of other woe

Than ours, a friend to man, to whom thou say'st,

Beauty is truth, truth beauty, – that is all

Ye know on earth, and all ye need to know.

Following pages:

Landscape with
Psyche outside the
Palace of Cupid
(The Enchanted
Castle) *by Claude
Lorrain (1647).
The painting inspired
the penultimate stanza
of Keats's 'Ode to a
Nightingale'.*

*The National Gallery,
London*

Finally, the 'Ode on Melancholy', with its conception of melancholy and delight dwelling together in human life, looks back to 'vale of soul making' passage in his letter to America:

She dwells with Beauty – Beauty that must die;

And Joy, whose hand is ever at his lips

Bidding adieu; and aching Pleasure nigh,

Turning to poison while the bee-mouth sips:

Ay, in the very temple of Delight

Veil'd Melancholy has her sovran shrine,

Though seen of none save him whose strenuous tongue

Can burst Joy's grape against his palate fine;

His soul shall taste the sadness of her might,

And be among her cloudy trophies hung.

In these great poems Keats finally achieved a perfect fusion of thought, form and expression. They are philosophic poems of power and immediacy, the crystallisation of the intellectual explorations recorded in the letters. In their dense shifting patterns we can trace every twist and turn of Keats's intense, restlessly enquiring mind.

~~~ *The Isle of Wight and Winchester: 1819*

T he calm spell at Wentworth Place was short-lived. On 13 May a disquieting letter arrived from America. Wilful as ever, George had changed his plans. He had invested his capital in a business venture in Kentucky and needed more money. Keats, with few funds of his own, was faced with the alarming possibility of having to find a job, something that would seriously disturb his programme of reading and writing. Perhaps, he thought, he could find work as a ship's surgeon. On top of this, Brown was, according to his custom, planning to rent his side of Wentworth Place for the summer, and so Keats urgently had to find somewhere to live. At the end of May he wrote to an old friend, Sarah Jeffrey, asking if she knew anywhere suitable in Teignmouth. 'I have the choice as it were of two Poisons,' he wrote, 'the one is voyaging to and from India for a few years, the other is leading a fevrous life alone with poetry.' But in truth he had already decided: 'This latter will suit me best,' he said, 'for I cannot resolve to give up my studies.'

Teignmouth, however, would always be associated with Tom. So when Keats received an invitation from James Rice to spend the summer on the Isle of Wight, the scene of his first attempts at *Endymion*, he was pleased to accept. As for the need to improve his financial situation, here he turned to the worldly Charles Brown for advice. Brown suggested that he write to the numerous friends who owed him money, asking for settlement. Keats was also persuaded, as he now told his sister, 'to try the press once more.' He would be going to the Isle of Wight with a clear purpose: 'to live cheaply in country and compose myself and verses as well as I can.' Brown's idea was that, between them, they would compose a play. He would provide the story and dramatic interest, and Keats would supply the verse. Before Keats left Hampstead they sketched out the broad idea: it was to be a tragedy set during the reign of Otho the Great, the first of the Holy Roman Emperors, and, most importantly, was to include a leading part worthy of the great Edmund Kean.

On 28 June, after a wet journey on the outside of the coach, Keats arrived at Shanklin, the village that had so delighted him two years earlier when he had come to begin *Endymion*. The following day he wrote, but did not send, a letter to Fanny Brawne. Two days later he tried again. It is clear that he was now very much in love:

> *I have never known any unalloy'd happiness for many days together: the death or sickness of some one has always spoilt my hours – and now when none such troubles oppress me, it is you must confess very hard that another sort of pain should haunt me. Ask yourself my love whether you are not very cruel to have so entrammelled me, so destroyed my freedom.*

Though his precarious financial situation ruled out marriage, by this time there seems to have been an 'understanding', if not an actual engagement, between him and Fanny.

For the next three weeks Keats wrote at an astonishing rate. By the time Brown had joined him at Shanklin in the middle of July, he had not only written the

Keats by Charles Brown, drawn in 1819 after the two friends had made a sketching trip to Shanklin Church on the Isle of Wight.

National Portrait Gallery, London

first act of *Otho the Great*, but had composed nearly four hundred lines of a new work, 'Lamia.' The poem recounts a story from one of Keats's favourite books, Robert Burton's *Anatomy of Melancholy*: Hermes gives human form to a serpent, who as a beautiful woman then ensnares a young philosopher, Lycius. It was written in tightly controlled rhyming couplets which owed a lot to the fluent, polished verse of the poet Keats was then reading closely, John Dryden. Keats's ambitions now had a harder, more professional edge. 'The Eve of St Agnes' and 'La Belle Dame Sans Merci' were trifles, the odes were private meditations, but 'Lamia' was, from the first, written to please the public and make money.

Brown's arrival was a relief. Ever since the journey, Keats had been suffering from a feverish cold and a severe sore throat, and in the poky cottage he and Rice, two invalids, had begun to try each other's nerves. Brown brought with him news of Fanny, some books and papers, as well as the manuscript of the still unfinished 'Hyperion', and together he and Keats continued with *Otho the Great*.

On 12 August Keats and Brown left the Isle of Wight and moved to Winchester. Keats hoped that the city would have the library he needed to complete the second and final part of 'Lamia.' At Winchester, which he found 'an exceedingly pleasant town,' he continued to work hard. 'I am convinced that more and more day by day that fine writing is next to fine doing the top thing in the world,' he wrote to Reynolds. He rapidly finished *Otho the Great*, and immediately began a new tragedy, *King Stephen*. Brown, who had suggested the subject, again offered to contribute, and later described Keats's forthright reaction: '"Stop!" he said, "stop! I have been already too long in leading-strings. I will do all this myself."' He had high hopes for this new play – 'One of my ambitions is to make as great a revolution in modern dramatic writing as Kean has done in acting,' he told Bailey – but after only a few scenes he dropped it. It had, like *Otho*, been intended for Kean, but while at Winchester he and Brown heard that the actor was about to tour America, and so would not be able to perform anything that season. Bitterly disappointed, Keats returned to 'Lamia', which he now finished, and then began to concentrate on gathering poems together for a new volume.

In September Brown departed. Left alone, Keats picked up the manuscript of 'Hyperion', and began radically to revise the long-unfinished epic. He now prefaced the poem with a long passage of great power, strongly influenced by his reading of Dante. The abstract nature of the original 'Hyperion' had been hard to sustain, and the tone was now more subjective. He was again trying to formulate a philosophy; what, he asks the goddess Moneta, makes him a poet, as distinct from a mere dreamer:

> *'If it please,*
>
> *Majestic shadow, tell me: sure not all*
>
> *Those melodies sung into the world's ear*
>
> *Are useless: sure a poet is a sage;*
>
> *A humanist, Physician to all men.*
>
> *That I am none I feel, as Vultures feel*
>
> *They are no birds when Eagles are abroad.*
>
> *What am I then? Thou spakest of my tribe:*
>
> *What tribe? – The tall shade veil'd in drooping white*
>
> *Then spake, so much more in earnest, that the breath*
>
> *Mov'd the thin folds that drooping hung*
>
> *About a golden censer from the hand*
>
> *Pendent. – Art thou not of the dreamer tribe?*
>
> *The poet and the dreamer are distinct,*
>
> *Diverse, sheer opposite, antipodes.*
>
> *The one pours out a balm upon the world,*
>
> *The other vexes it.*

Work on 'The Fall of Hyperion: A Dream', as the revised poem came to be called, was interrupted when, on 10 September, another letter arrived from George, urgently requesting money. Forced to break away from this new poetry, Keats left Winchester and went immediately to London. He stayed for five hectic days: he talked with Woodhouse about the poems for his proposed new volume, saw his sister Fanny at Walthamstow and talked with Abbey. He could not, however, bring himself to go to Hampstead and see Fanny Brawne. 'Am I mad or not?' he asked her in a letter. 'If I were to see you to day it would destroy the half-

Season of Mists and mellow fruitfulness
Close bosom friend of the maturing sun;
Conspiring with him how to load and bless
The Vines with fruit that round the thatch eves run.
To bend with apples the mossd Cottage trees
And fill all fruits with sweetness to the core
To swell the gourd, and plump the hazle shells
With a white kernel, to set budding more
And still more, later flowers for the bees,
Until they think warm days will never cease
For Summer has o'er brimm'd their clammy cells.

By anyra thy stores?
Who hath not seen thee? ~~for thee haunts the way~~
                                                abroad
Sometimes whoever seeks ~~for thee~~ may find
Thee sitting ~~careless~~ on a granary floom
Thy hair soft lifted by the winnowing wing
                                        hurthys
~~While bright the bees slants through the barn;~~
~~on on a half reap'd furrow sound asleep~~
~~Or sound asleep in a half reaped field~~

Dosed with red poppies, while thy reeping hook
~~Spares from some slumbrous~~ warm slumbers creep
                    minutes while warm
Or on a half reap'd furrow sound asleep
Dos'd with the fume of poppies, while thy hook
~~Spares the next swath, and all its fringed flowers~~
~~Spares for some slumbrous minutes the next swath;~~

And sometimes like a gleaner thou dost keep
Steady thy laden head across the brook,
Or by a Cyder-press with patent look
Thou watchest the last oozing hours by hours

comfortable sullenness I enjoy at present into downright perplexities. I love you too much to venture into Hampstead, I feel it is not paying a visit, but venturing into a fire.'

On 15 September Keats returned to Winchester. There resuming his daily routine of writing, reading and walking, he regained his emotional balance. He found the approaching autumn particularly calming. 'How beautiful the season is now,' he wrote to Reynolds on 21 September. 'How fine the air. A temperate sharpness about it. Really, without joking, chaste weather – Dian skies – I never lik'd stubble fields so much as now – Aye better than the chilly green of the spring. Somehow a stubble plain looks warm – in the same way that some pictures look warm – This struck me so much in my sunday's walk that I composed upon it.' The composition was his last truly great poem, the serene ode, 'To Autumn'

Opposite page:

The manuscript of Keats's last great ode, 'To Autumn', written at Winchester in September 1819.

The Houghton Library, Harvard University, Massachusetts

Where are the songs of Spring? Ay, where are they?
Think not of them, thou hast thy music too, -
While barred clouds bloom the soft-dying day,
And touch the stubble plain with rosy hue;
Then in a wailful choir the small gnats mourn
Among the river sallows, borne aloft
Or sinking as the light wind lives or dies;
And full-grown lambs loud bleat from hilly bourn;
Hedge-crickets sing; and now with treble soft
The red-breast whistles from a garden-croft;
And gathering swallows twitter in the skies

Final Months in England: 1819–20

Keats returned to London on 8 October 1819. It had been a remarkably creative year. In the space of twelve months Keats had composed almost all the works for which he is now famous, and which have earned him a place, as he had hoped, 'among the English poets': 'Hyperion', 'The Eve of St. Agnes', 'La Belle Dame sans Merci', 'Lamia' and the great odes. But from Keats's own point of view it had been a terrible year. His youngest brother had died an agonising death, and his surviving brother had emigrated and run into grave financial difficulties; his one substantial published work, *Endymion*, had received appalling reviews, and his second attempt at epic, 'Hyperion', remained unfinished. 'I have given up Hyperion,' he had written to Reynolds from Winchester, 'there were too many Miltonic inversions in it – Miltonic verse cannot be written but in an artful or rather artist's humour. I wish to give myself up to other sensations. English ought to be kept up.' 'Nothing could have in all its circumstances fallen out worse for me than the last year has done', he wrote bitterly to George and Georgiana, 'or could be more damping to my poetical talent.'

Then there was his love for Fanny Brawne. The previous November he had told his brother and sister-in-law that marriage would only distract him from his imaginative and poetic life. Now he found himself in the grip of emotions which directly challenged that view. On his return to London he put off going to Hampstead, and lodged instead in Westminster; 'I like Miss Brawne and I cannot help it' he had written to Brown from Hampstead. 'On that account I had better not live there.' When, on 10 October, he did finally visit Wentworth Place, the effect was overpowering: 'You dazzled me –' he wrote afterwards to her, 'There is nothing in the world so bright and delicate … When shall we pass a day alone?' Two days later he wrote again:

> *You have ravish'd me away by a Power I cannot resist, and yet I could resist till I saw you; and ever since I have seen you I have endeavoured often ìto reason against the reasons of my loveî. I can do that no more – the pain would be too great – My love is selfish – I cannot breathe without you.*

A miniature of Fanny Brawne, made in about 1833, twelve years after Keats's death. Artist unknown.

Keats House, London

This capacity for intense emotion was something Keats had always recognised in himself. 'I carry all matters to an extreme,' he had confided to Bailey from Scotland, 'so that when I have any little vexation it grows in five Minutes into a theme for Sophocles.' Fanny, still only eighteen, must have been somewhat overwhelmed by being such an object of devotion, but in later life she looked at this side of Keats's character with an astute and sympathetic eye; 'That his sensibility was most acute, is true,' she wrote, 'and his passions were very strong, but not violent, if by that term violence of temper is implied. His was no doubt susceptible, his anger seemed rather to turn on himself than others, and in moments of greatest irritation, it was only by a sort of savage despondency that he sometimes wounded his friends. Violence … was quite foreign to his nature.'

Towards the end of October Keats did in the end move back to Wentworth to live again with Brown. He gave Fanny a garnet ring, and there was probably some kind of formal engagement. But his lack of financial stability ruled out any chance of a foreseeable marriage, and Fanny's proximity next door only heightened his frustration. Brown, meanwhile, was conducting an amorous affair with their housekeeper, Abigail O'Donaghue. 'The very kindness of his friends was at this time felt to be oppressive to him,' wrote Dilke later of Keats, '… from this period his weakness & his sufferings mental & bodily, increased – his whole mind & heart were in a whirl of contending passions – he saw nothing calmly or dispassionately.'

Keats's intentions as a writer were in a similar state of unrest. His aim in Winchester had been to gather his recent poetry together to form a new volume. But in November he wrote to Taylor to say that he would not, in fact, publish anything that he had written since *Endymion*; instead he promised a new, much finer poem, with perhaps two or three more poems, 'if God should spare me', over the next six years, and then 'the writing of a few fine plays – my greatest ambition.' Then he changed his mind again, and spent the later part of November and early December preparing his existing poems for the press. He also began a new poem, a satirical comedy entitled 'The Cap and Bells.' By 20 December he was optimistic again: 'My hopes of success in the literary world are now better than ever,' he told his sister Fanny; a few days later he told Brown of his intention to earn money as a journalist; 'by prosing awhile in periodical works I may maintain myself decently', he said.

In the new year his brother George arrived from America. He was, as usual, badly in need of money, and for the next month was busy with business meetings and parties. As devoted as always, the two brothers spent all their time together, and when he left at the beginning of February George took with him a notebook containing copies of Keats's recent poems.

Two days after George's departure, Keats suffered a misfortune which was to change his life for ever. The night was bitter, and as Keats returned from town, as usual in the cheap seats on the outside of the coach, he caught a severe cold. Seeing him stumble into Wentworth Place at eleven o'clock at night, Brown thought for a moment that he was drunk, but quickly realised that he was in fact seriously ill and immediately helped him up to bed. What happened next is unforgettably described in Brown's own words:

Keats's 'Ode on a Grecian Urn', in the hand of his brother George Keats, one of the poems that his brother copied into a notebook to take back with him to America in 1820.

The British Library, London Egerton MS 2780 f.55

On entering the cold sheets, before his head was on the pillow, he slightly coughed, and I heard him say, – 'That is blood from my mouth.' I went towards him; he was examining a single drop of blood upon the sheet. 'Bring me the candle Brown; and let me see this blood.' After regarding it steadfastly, he looked up in my face, with a calmness that I can never forget, and said –'I know the colour of that blood; – it is arterial blood; – I cannot be deceived in that colour; – that drop of blood is my death warrant; – I must die.'

Keats had, he knew, suffered a haemorrhage. It was an early sign of tuberculosis, the family curse that had taken the lives of his mother and brother. That night he had a second, massive haemorrhage. 'This is unfortunate,' he choked as he struggled for breath. 'On the night I was taken ill when so violent a rush of blood came to my Lungs that I felt nearly suffocated,' he wrote afterwards to Fanny Brawne. 'I assure you I felt it possible I might not survive and at that moment thought of nothing but you.'

Keats was now confined to the house. A sick bed was set up, and he was left to brood upon what had just happened. Fanny Brawne sometimes came to visit, but they mainly communicated through a succession of notes, often no more than a simple 'Good night' which Keats would place under his pillow. A succession of well-meaning visitors called, and Keats remarked wryly to his sister, 'I have had so many presents of jam and jellies that they would read side by side the length of the sideboard.' His mind went right back to his early days in rural Enfield. 'How astonishingly does the chance of leaving the world impress a sense of its natural beauties upon us,' he wrote to James Rice. 'I muse with the greatest affection on every flower I have known from my infancy – their shapes and colours are as new to me as if I had just created them with a superhuman fancy – It is because they are connected with the most thoughtless and happiest moments of our Lives – I have seen foreign flowers in hothouses of the most beautiful nature, but I do not care a straw for them. The simple flowers of our spring are what I want to see again.' Then he mused upon his achievements as a poet, and wrote philosophically to Fanny Brawne:

> 'If I should die', said I to myself, 'I have left no immortal work behind me – nothing to make my friends proud of my memory – but I have lov'd the principle of beauty in all things, and if I had had time I would have made myself remembered.'

So life continued for the rest of February and into March, with Keats, as he put it to Dilke, 'gradually, too gradually perhaps, improving.' His work on the forthcoming volume was delayed at the beginning March by 'violent palpitations of the heart', but he soon rallied and, Brown told Taylor optimistically, 'we are now assured there is no pulmunary affection; no organic defect whatever.' On 25 March he was sufficiently well to attend the viewing of Haydon's *Christ's Triumphal Entry into Jerusalem*, which the painter had finally finished. There he talked with Hazlitt, and afterwards managed to walk the six miles back to Wentworth Place without any noticeable ill effect. A month later, he presented the manuscript of the new volume to his publishers.

In May, according to his custom, Brown made arrangements to rent out his half of Wentworth Place. And so, once again, Keats was faced with having to find somewhere to live during the summer. This time help came from his old friend Leigh Hunt, who found him comfortable enough lodgings at Kentish Town, only a few doors away from his own home. There he lay on his makeshift bed and stared obsessively in the direction of Hampstead. The frustration became unbearable. He sent a number of violently possessive letters to Fanny, then immediately followed them with heartfelt apologies; 'My fairest, my delicious, my angel Fanny!', he wrote in June, 'Do not believe me such a vulgar fellow. I will be as patient in illness and as believing in Love as I am able.' His feelings for women had always been complicated. 'I am certain I have not a right feeling towards Women,' he had written to Bailey in 1818. 'Is it because they fall so far beneath my Boyish imagination? … I thought them etherial above Men – I find them perhaps equal – great by comparison is very small.' But whereas before the complexities of his intense nature had been tempered by generosity, intellectual energy and humour, they were now exacerbated by illness and frustrated love.

At Kentish Town he worked on the printer's proofs for the forthcoming volume with mixed feelings – 'My book is coming out with very low hopes, though not spirits on my part. This shall be my last trial; not succeeding, I shall try what I can do in the Apothecary line.' One day Hunt accompanied Keats on a coach ride through the countryside around Hampstead, and his spirits seemed to improve. 'It was nevertheless on the same day,' Hunt later wrote, 'sitting on the bench in Well Walk, at Hampstead, nearest the heath, that he told me, with unaccustomed tears in his eyes, that "his heart was breaking".'

Later that month Keats suffered another haemorrhage. As before, this was followed by a further haemorrhage of much greater violence. Still spitting blood, he was immediately moved into Hunt's noisy, chaotic house. It was now agreed that he would have to go to a warmer climate if he was to survive the winter. 'He is advised – nay ordered – to go to Italy,' wrote Reynolds pessimistically, 'but in such a state it is a hopeless doom.' Joseph Severn called, and was shocked at Keats's appearance:

LAMIA,

ISABELLA,

THE EVE OF ST. AGNES,

AND

OTHER POEMS.

BY JOHN KEATS,

AUTHOR OF ENDYMION.

LONDON:
PRINTED FOR TAYLOR AND HESSEY,
FLEET-STREET.
1820.

Keats's last collection,
Lamia, Isabella, the
Eve of St. Agnes, and
Other Poems, *was
published by Taylor and
Hessey in 1820.
It contains most of
Keats's greatest poetry.*

*The British Library, London
C39 b 67*

'Poor Keats is still nearer the next world,' he wrote. 'His appearance is shocking and now reminds me of poor Tom – and I have been inclined to think him in the same way – for himself – he makes sure of it – and seems prepossessed that he cannot recover.'

At the beginning of July Keats's third volume, *Lamia, Isabella, The Eve of St. Agnes, and Other Poems*, was published; 'if it does not sell well, I think that nothing will ever sell again,' Taylor wrote to his father, 'I am sure of this that for poetic genius

Isabella *by Sir John Everett Millais, a painting inspired by Keats's poem of the same name.*

A self-portrait of Keats's friend Joseph Severn, who accompanied him to Italy.

National Portrait Gallery, London

there is not his equal living.' This time, there were a number of favourable notices. Writing in the *New Times*, Charles Lamb picked out 'Isabella' and 'The Eve of St. Agnes' for particular praise, writing of the latter: 'like the radiance, which comes from those old windows upon the limbs and garments of the damsel, is the almost Chaucer-like painting, with which this poet illumines every subject he touches. We have scarcely anything like it in modern description.' 'My book has had a good success among literary people,' Keats wrote in August, 'and, I believe, has a moderate sale.'

Meanwhile he continued to live at Hunt's, thinking constantly of Fanny. On 12 August he received a letter from Percy Bysshe Shelley, inviting him to stay with him in Italy: 'I think you would do well to pass the winter after so tremendous an accident in Italy,' Shelley wrote from Pisa. 'Mrs Shelley unites with myself in urging the request, that you would take up your residence with us.' It was a generous offer, but Keats was hesitant. Then, later that day, he was given a letter from Fanny Brawne; he saw that it had been sent two days ago, and the seal had been broken. His nerves, under immense strain for so long, finally snapped. Ill as he was, he dragged himself out of the house and made for Hampstead. He was seen standing at the end of Well Walk, sobbing uncontrollably into a handkerchief. That evening he knocked on the door of Wentworth Place and, after one look at his desperate appearance, the Brawnes took him in.

Keats spent the next month with the Brawnes. 'I am excessively nervous,' he wrote to his sister, 'a person I am not quite used to entering the room half choaks me.' The prospect of going abroad distressed him, but he began to think of how to finance a trip to Italy, and wrote to Taylor for advice. His considerate publisher at once set about making the arrangements, and settled on Rome as the best destination. Keats hoped that Brown would accompany him, but was unable to reach him in Scotland. In September, Joseph Severn was asked if he would undertake this difficult task, and immediately accepted.

Keats spent his final days in England making his farewells. He exchanged locks of hair and gifts with Fanny Brawne; he gave her the miniature of him by Severn, while she gave him a pocket diary and a penknife. He dictated to her a letter to his sister: 'In the hope of entirely re-establishing my health,' he wrote. 'I shall leave England for Italy this week and, of course I shall not be able to see you before my departure ... You shall hear from me as often as possible, if I feel too tired to write myself I shall have some friend to do it for me.' Other friends made their farewell, and Fanny Brawne was astonished by the devotion that Keats seemed to inspire: 'I am certain he has some spell that attaches them to him,' she wrote to Fanny Keats, 'or else he has fortunately met with a circle of friends that I did not believe could be found in the world.'

On the 17 September, Keats and Severn boarded the *Maria Crowther* at the London Docks. The following night they set sail for Italy.

A lock of Keats's hair; 'if you placed your hand upon his head' his friend Benjamin Bailey wrote in 1849, 'the silken curls felt like the rich plumage of a bird.'

*The British Library, London
Ashley MS 4870*

111

≋ *Italy: 1820–21*

For two weeks the *Maria Crowther* inched slowly and painfully along the English coast. Storms flooded the ship, and made everyone seasick. Then came a dead calm that played terribly upon Keats's nerves. The single cabin was tiny, and was shared between Keats, Severn, the captain, and two female passengers: a Mrs Pidgeon, and eighteen-year old Miss Cotterell, also suffering from tuberculosis. After ten days the ship reached Portsmouth, and here Keats and Severn went ashore. They learned that by an extraordinary coincidence, Brown had left Scotland and was now nearby in Chichester. It was an opportunity for Keats to abandon the voyage and return to London, but he decided against it. Whatever the state of his health, to return to Wentworth Place and Fanny Brawne would now be unbearable. 'Were I in health it would make ill, and how can I bear it my state?' he explained to Brown. 'The thought of leaving Miss Brawne is beyond everything horrible – The sense of darkness coming over me – I eternally see her figure eternally vanishing ... Is there another life? Shall I awake and find all this a dream? There must be we cannot be created for this sort of suffering.'

At last fair winds came, and the ship escaped the English coastline and headed out to sea. At first Keats's health seemed to improve – 'quite the "special person" of olden time' wrote Severn – but two days past the Straits of Gibraltar he had another severe haemorrhage, and became feverous. His fellow consumptive, Miss Cotterell, was not helping matters, for though suffering from the same disease as Keats, she had opposite needs. If the cabin window was closed, for example, she would faint and lie insensible for several hours; but if the windows were open, Keats was racked with uncontrollable coughing.

On 21 October, after three weeks at sea, the *Maria Crowther* reached the Bay of Naples. Here the passengers learned that because of a typhus epidemic in London, a quarantine had been imposed on all incoming ships. They now had to stay on board ship for a further ten days. Sitting on deck, surrounded by two thousand other ships, Keats would look towards Mount Vesuvius 'with so sad a look in his eyes' wrote Severn, 'with, moreover, sometimes, a starved haunting expression that bewildered me.' He wrote a letter to Mrs Brawne, saying how he could not wait to see the back

One of Keats's final letters, to Charles Brown, 30 September 1820, written on board the Maria Crowther *off the Isle of Wight.*

The Houghton Library, Harvard University, Massachusetts

of Miss Cotterell, and finally be free of the ship. He did not dare to think of Fanny, he said, but he cherished her final gifts to him. He wanted to give Mrs Brawne a fine description of the Bay of Naples, but he was simply too ill: 'O what an account I could give you if I could once more feel myself a Citizen of this world … what a misery it is to have an intellect in splints!' he wrote. Finally, at the very bottom of the page and in tiny letters, he wrote his last words to Fanny: 'Good bye Fanny! god bless you.'

On 31 October the passengers were finally released from quarantine. Severn was surprised that Keats had survived it. They took a large, airy room with fine views, and spent a few days looking around Naples. Miss Cotterell's brother, a resident of the city, acted as their guide. Keats was at his lowest; 'Oh Brown, I have coals of fire in my breast,' he wrote. 'It surprised me that the human heart is capable of containing and bearing so much misery. Was I born for this end?'

On 7 November Keats and Severn left for Rome. There was little Severn could do to ease his friend's discomfort except walk by the side of the coach to give him more room. As he walked he gathered armfuls of wild flowers to brighten the cabin. A week later they reached Rome, and were met by an English doctor, James Clarke, who installed them in a second-floor apartment on the Piazza di Spagna. The rooms pleased Keats; they were quiet, and at night he could hear the soothing sounds of a fountain. Rome itself entranced him, and he spent several days looking around the city with a young English army officer, Lieutenant Isaac Elton, who was also suffering from consumption. A sign of the old humour returned one day, when, in protest at the appalling quality of the food, he calmly emptied an entire meal, dish by dish, out of the window. 'This was all done to the amusement of the porter and padrona,' Severn later recalled, 'he then quietly but very decidedly pointed to the basket for the porter to take away, which he did without demur. "Now," said Keats, "you'll see, Severn, that we'll have an excellent dinner;" and sure enough in less than half-an-hour an excellent one came, and we continued to be similarly well treated every day.'

On 30 November he wrote another, more measured letter to Brown: ''tis the most difficult thing in the world for me to write a letter,' he began, 'yet I am much better than I was in Quarantine ... I have an habitual feeling of my life having past, and that I am leading a posthumous existence.' He spoke of his regret at their missing each other at Portsmouth, and asked Brown to write to George, and 'also a note to my sister – who walks about my imagination like a ghost – she is so like Tom.' After asking after a number of his friends, he movingly closes what was to be his final letter: 'I can scarcely bid you goodbye even in a letter. I always made an awkward bow. God bless you!'

On 10 December Keats had a final relapse. Over the next nine days he suffered five haemorrhages. Severn nursed him constantly, reading to him by day, and sitting up with him while his fevered mind wandered at night. As his condition worsened, Keats grew intent on ending his own life; on 17 December he rushed out of bed crying 'This day shall be my last.' Severn, however, managed to keep every means of suicide out of his reach. Letters arrived from England, but Keats was unable to read them – 'they tear him to pieces', Severn said. Any reminder of his past life was too much for him and the promise of death became his only comfort.

The Spanish Steps in Rome by Maria Lady Callcott. Keats and Severn lodged in the right-hand building on the second floor. The house is now a memorial to the poet.

The British Museum, London

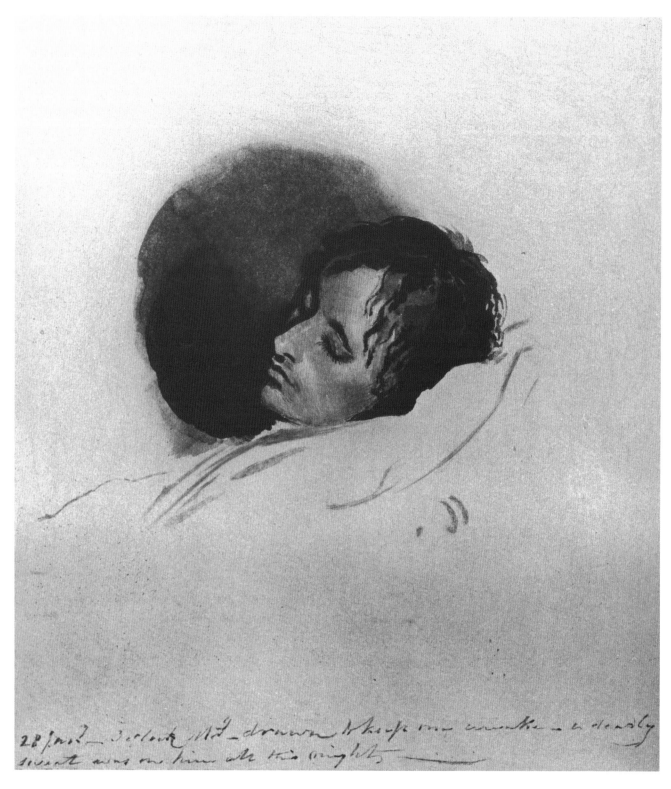

28 Jan.— 3 oclock Md— drawn Wheap my cweether— a deadly
sweat was on him all this night.—— —

Every day he would fix Clarke with a terrible, hollow-eyed stare and demand: 'how long will this posthumous existence of mine last?'; 'that look was more than we could ever bear,' Severn wrote, 'the extreme brightness of his eyes – with his poor pallid face – were not earthly.'

On 21 February he thought the end had come. He asked Severn to lift him up in bed: 'did you ever see anyone die', he asked, 'well then I pity you poor Severn … I shall soon be laid in the quiet grave, thank God for the quiet grave – O! I can feel the cold earth upon me – the daisies growing over me – O for this quiet – it will be my first.' When the morning came and he found that he was still alive he wept.

Two days later, at four in the afternoon, Keats suddenly spoke: 'Severn – I – lift me up – I am dying – I shall die easy – don't be frightened – be firm, and thank God it has come!' For the next seven hours he lay in Severn's arms, breathing with the utmost difficulty, the phlegm seeming to boil in his throat. He spoke only once more – 'don't breathe on me – it comes like Ice.' At eleven o'clock that night he died, so quietly that Severn thought he had fallen asleep.

Opposite page:

Keats on his deathbed by Joseph Severn. The inscription reads: '28 January, 1821, 3 o'clock morning, drawn to keep me awake. A deadly sweat was on him all this night'.

Keats House, London

✒ *Epilogue*

John Keats was buried at dawn on 26 February 1821 at the Protestant Cemetery in Rome. His last gifts and letters from Fanny Brawne and his sister were buried with him. Dr Clarke placed turfs of daisies over the grave, and in the coming months Severn would often visit the site; 'I walked there a few days ago,' he wrote, 'and found the daisies had grown all over it. It is one of the most lovely retired spots in Rome … with no sound in the air but the tinkling of a few simple sheep and goats.' Keats had wished his gravestone to say simply: 'Here lies one whose name was writ in water'. Brown, however, added a preface: 'This Grave contains all that was Mortal, of a young English Poet Who, on his Death Bed in the Bitterness of his heart at the Malicious Power of his enemies, Desired these Words to be engraven on his Tomb Stone'.

When Shelley heard the news in Pisa he was moved to write one of his finest poems, the great elegy, 'Adonais.' A year later, he too was dead, drowned in a storm off the coast of Lerici. A copy of Keats's *Lamia* volume was found in his pocket. His ashes were buried next to Keats in the Protestant Cemetery.

When Fanny Brawne was told the news she went into deep and prolonged mourning. In the coming years Keats's sister, Fanny, became one of her closest friends and confidantes. George Keats's fortunes in America changed for the better, and he became a wealthy citizen of Louisville, Kentucky before his sudden death from tuberculosis in 1841. Of the four Keats children, only Fanny lived into old age; in 1833 she married a Spaniard, Valentin Llanos, and spent the remainder of her long life in Spain. Keats's friends soon went their separate ways after his death. Without exception however, they treasured their friendship with Keats as one of the greatest periods of their lives.

It was not until the Victorian age, and the publication of Richard Monckton Milnes's biography in 1848, that Keats's poetry attracted the attention it deserved. Tennyson and Browning were both inspired by his work; 'He would have been among the very greatest of us if he had lived', said Tennyson. 'There is something of the innermost soul of poetry in almost everything he ever wrote.' The Pre-Raphaelite painters ranked him on a par with Dante, Homer, Chaucer and Goethe.

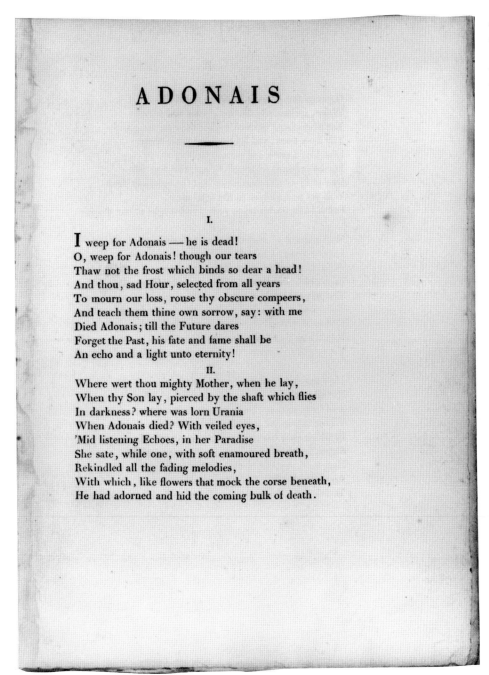

ADONAIS

—

I.

I weep for Adonais —— he is dead!
O, weep for Adonais! though our tears
Thaw not the frost which binds so dear a head!
And thou, sad Hour, selected from all years
To mourn our loss, rouse thy obscure compeers,
And teach them thine own sorrow, say: with me
Died Adonais; till the Future dares
Forget the Past, his fate and fame shall be
An echo and a light unto eternity!

II.

Where wert thou mighty Mother, when he lay,
When thy Son lay, pierced by the shaft which flies
In darkness? where was lorn Urania
When Adonais died? With veiled eyes,
'Mid listening Echoes, in her Paradise
She sate, while one, with soft enamoured breath,
Rekindled all the fading melodies,
With which, like flowers that mock the corse beneath,
He had adorned and hid the coming bulk of death.

Today, Keats is recognised as one the great poets of the Romantic, or indeed any age, confirmation of his own sure assertion: 'I think I shall be among the English Poets after my death.'

John Keats 1795–1821
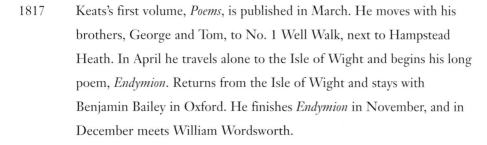 *Chronology*

1795   John Keats is born in London on 31 October.

1803-11   Keats enters John Clarke's school at Enfield.

1804   Death of Keats's father, Thomas. His mother remarries.

1810   Death of Keats's mother of tuberculosis.

1811   Keats leaves Enfield School and begins an apprenticeship with Thomas
          Hammond, a surgeon at Edmonton.

1814   Keats writes his first known poem, 'Imitation of Spenser'.

1815   Keats enters Guy's Hospital as a medical student.

1816   'O Solitude', Keats's first published poem, appears in *The Examiner*.
          In July he passes the examination at Apothecaries' Hall, thus becoming
          eligible to practise as an apothecary. In October he writes his first great
          sonnet, 'On First looking into Chapman's Homer'. He makes many new
          friends, and gives up medicine for poetry.

1817   Keats's first volume, *Poems*, is published in March. He moves with his
          brothers, George and Tom, to No. 1 Well Walk, next to Hampstead
          Heath. In April he travels alone to the Isle of Wight and begins his long
          poem, *Endymion*. Returns from the Isle of Wight and stays with
          Benjamin Bailey in Oxford. He finishes *Endymion* in November, and in
          December meets William Wordsworth.

1818   In January and February Keats regularly goes to hear Hazlitt lecture on the English poets. Tom Keats begins to show signs of having tuberculosis. In February he begins 'Isabella, or The Pot of Basil'. *Endymion* is published in March. In May George Keats marries and emigrates to America.

      Over the summer Keats and Brown tour the Lake District and Scotland. That autumn, *Endymion* is savagely reviewed in the Tory periodicals. Keats meets Fanny Brawne and begins 'Hyperion'. On 1 December Tom Keats dies, and Keats goes to live with Brown at Wentworth Place, Hampstead.

1819   Keats's most productive year as a poet. In January he goes to Chichester and writes 'The Eve of St. Agnes'. Between April and May, at Wentworth Place, he writes 'La Belle Dame Sans Merci' and the great odes: 'To a Nightingale', 'On a Grecian Urn', 'On Melancholy'.

      In the summer he goes to the Isle of Wight and writes a play, *Otho the Great*, and completes half of 'Lamia'. In September he is at Winchester with Charles Brown, where he finishes 'Lamia', revises 'Hyperion' (now called 'The Fall of Hyperion, A Dream') and writes 'To Autumn'.

1820   In February Keats has a severe haemorrhage. From this time his health steadily declines, and by the end of the year he is seriously ill with tuberculosis. He becomes engaged to Fanny Brawne. His final volume, *Lamia, Isabella, The Eve of St. Agnes and Other Poems* is published in July. By this time Keats has been ordered to spend the winter in Italy. In September, accompanied by Severn, he sails for Italy, arriving in Naples on 21 October. In November Keats and Severn move to Rome, where they lodge on the Piazza di Spagna. Keats is attended by a British physician, Dr James Clark.

1821   On 23 February John Keats dies at 11 pm. He is buried at the Protestant Cemetery in Rome. News of his death reaches England on 17 March.

Further Reading

Original Works

Poems:

The Poems of John Keats, ed. Miriam Allott (Longman, 1972)

John Keats, The Complete Poems, ed. John Barnard (Penguin, 1977)

John Keats, Complete Poems, ed. Jack Stillinger
(Harvard University Press, 1982)

Letters:

The Letters of John Keats, ed. Hyder E. Rollins
(Harvard University Press, 1958)

John Keats, Selected Letters, ed. Robert Gittings
(Oxford University Press, 2002)

Selected Poems and Letters of Keats, ed. Robert Gittings (Heinemann, 1992)

Biography

John Keats, Walter Jackson Bate (Harvard University Press, 1979)

John Keats, The Living Year, Robert Gittings (Heinemann, 1954)

John Keats, Robert Gittings (Penguin, 2001)

Keats, Andrew Motion (Faber, 1997)

John Keats, The Making of a Poet, Aileen Ward (Secker and Warburg, 1963)

Other works

The Immortal Dinner, Penelope Hughes-Hallett (Penguin, 2001)

Keats and the Mirror of Art, Ian Jack (Oxford, 1967)

Keats and Embarrassment, Christopher Ricks (Oxford, 1974)

John Keats and the Culture of Dissent, Nicholas Roe (Clarendon Press, 1997)

❧ *Index*

The British Library is grateful to Abbot Hall, Kendal; The Bridgeman Art Library, London; The British Museum, London; Fitzwilliam Museum, Cambridge; Guildhall Library, London; Harvard University, Massachusetts; Keats House, London; Keats-Shelley House, Rome; The National Gallery, London; The National Portrait Gallery, London; New York Public Library; Victoria & Albert Museum, London; Walker Art Gallery, Merseyside; Whitworth Art Gallery, Manchester; The Wordsworth Trust, Grasmere; Yale Center for British Art and other named copyright holders for permission to reproduce illustrations.

Front cover illustrations:	Keats by Joseph Severn (Wordsworth Trust), *The Vale of Health on Hampstead Heath* by George Shepherd (Victoria & Albert Museum), *Hyperion* (The British Library, Add. MS 37000 f.1)
Back cover illustrations:	Keats by Joseph Severn (National Portrait Gallery, London), *A view of Windermere* by J.M.W. Turner (Bridgeman Art Library/ Abbot Hall, Kendal)
Half title page:	*John Keats* by Girometti (Keats House)
Frontispiece:	'Ode on a Grecian Urn' (The British Library, Egerton MS 2780 f.55)
Contents page:	Wentworth Place (Keats House)

Text © 2002 Stephen Hebron

Illustrations © 2002 The British Library Board and other named copyright holders

Published in the United States of America by
Oxford University Press, Inc.
198 Madison Avenue,
New York, NY 10016
www.oup.com

Oxford is a registered trademark of Oxford University Press, Inc.

ISBN 0-19-521787-X

First published 2002 by The British Library, 96 Euston Road, London NW1 2DB

Designed and typeset by Crayon Design, Stoke Row, Henley-on-Thames
Map by John Mitchell
Colour and black-and-white origination by Crayon Design and South Sea International Press
Printed in Hong Kong by South Sea International Press